HOW TO MANAGE DEPRESSION

Dr. Maxwell Shimba

SHIMBA
PUBLISHING

TABLE OF CONTENTS

INTRODUCTION

Understanding and Managing Depression

Depression is one of the most widespread mental health challenges today, touching the lives of millions of people across all walks of life. It transcends boundaries of age, race, and social background, affecting the rich and the poor, the young and the elderly alike. For many, it becomes an invisible weight, a burden that can feel inescapable and isolating. Those who face depression may feel trapped in cycles of sadness, exhaustion, and hopelessness, often without a clear reason why.

Despite how common depression is, it remains deeply misunderstood. Depression is not simply "feeling sad" or "going through a rough patch." It's a complex, multifaceted condition that involves changes in how the brain functions, affecting mood, energy, sleep, and even physical health. Many people with depression struggle to find the motivation to engage in daily tasks, let alone seek treatment. But it's important to remember that depression is a treatable condition, and with the right support, people can and do recover.

A Holistic Approach to Healing

Managing depression requires a compassionate and comprehensive approach that addresses the many layers of the condition. In recent years, our understanding of depression has expanded to include biological, psychological, social, and even spiritual dimensions. We now recognize that overcoming depression often involves more than just one strategy or a single form of treatment; rather, it requires an approach that respects both the science of the mind and the wisdom of the soul.

In this book, we'll explore how various strategies—ranging from physical health practices to cognitive therapies—can work together to help manage depression. We'll examine the value of exercise, proper sleep, nutrition, and social connection in supporting mental health. But we'll also look at the spiritual aspects of recovery, tapping into the comfort and strength that faith and spirituality can offer to those struggling with depression.

Throughout this book, we will draw on both psychological theories and theological perspectives to offer a balanced view. Psychological science provides us with evidence-based methods, such as Cognitive Behavioral Therapy (CBT), to address the negative thought patterns that often accompany depression. Theological insights, on the other hand, offer hope, purpose, and a framework for understanding suffering and healing. Together, these approaches aim to provide a more complete, nurturing path to mental wellness.

The Structure of the Book

This book is divided into several chapters, each focused on a different aspect of managing depression.

1. Understanding Depression: We begin by defining depression, exploring its symptoms, causes, and effects on daily life. This chapter will also cover major psychological theories to deepen our understanding of depression and its roots.

2. The Power of Physical Health: Next, we'll dive into the role of exercise, sleep, and nutrition. Simple, healthy routines can be transformative, improving mood, energy levels, and even overall mental clarity.

3. Social Connection and Support: Human beings are social creatures, and connecting with others plays a vital role in emotional resilience. Here, we'll discuss practical ways to reach out, as well as the importance of communities of faith and friends.

4. Avoiding Harmful Substances and Habits: Many people with depression turn to substances like alcohol or tobacco to cope, which can worsen their symptoms. We'll look at healthier alternatives and strategies to avoid these harmful habits.

5. Strengthening the Mind through Cognitive Techniques: This chapter introduces Cognitive Behavioral Therapy (CBT), a powerful tool for managing depression by helping individuals reshape their thought patterns and behaviors.

6. The Healing Light of Sunlight and Nature: Spending time in natural settings and getting enough sunlight can have profound effects on mood. We'll explore ways to incorporate these elements into daily life.

7. Faith, Prayer, and Spiritual Practice: Spirituality and faith can offer deep comfort, hope, and a sense of purpose during dark times. This chapter will delve into the benefits of prayer, meditation, and other spiritual practices.

8. Psychological and Medical Interventions: In cases where depression is more severe, additional treatments like medication or Electroconvulsive Therapy (ECT) may be recommended. Here, we'll discuss these options, along with any misconceptions surrounding them.

Each chapter will include practical exercises, questions for reflection, and insights drawn from both scientific research and religious teachings. This holistic approach not only addresses the physical and mental dimensions of depression but also seeks to heal the soul.

Why Psychological and Theological Perspectives Matter

Combining psychological theories with theological perspectives offers a unique, well-rounded approach to understanding and managing depression. Psychology provides practical tools and scientifically grounded therapies, but it can sometimes lack the depth of meaning that people need when facing profound suffering. Theology and spirituality, on the other hand, address questions of purpose, existence, and hope, reminding us that we are more than our struggles. Together, these disciplines can provide both practical steps and lasting comfort, creating a space where people can explore their emotional health within the framework of a higher purpose or divine love.

Throughout this journey, remember that you are not alone. You are embarking on a path that millions of others have walked, supported by tools that have helped countless people find healing and peace. Whether your hope is rooted in faith, psychology, or both, this book aims to offer a supportive companion for your healing journey. Depression may be a formidable challenge, but with courage, compassion, and the right resources, a life of peace, joy, and fulfillment is possible.

xi

DR. MAXWELL SHIMBA

CHAPTER 01

UNDERSTANDING DEPRESSION

Depression is a term that many people use casually, often to describe a passing feeling of sadness or disappointment. However, clinical depression is far more profound and complex, affecting millions of people across the world with symptoms that go well beyond occasional feelings of sadness. Depression is a serious mental health condition that impacts a person's mood, thoughts, physical health, and day-to-day functioning. This chapter explores what depression is, outlines the different types of depression, and helps clarify why understanding this condition is so essential to managing it effectively.

What is Depression?

At its core, depression is a persistent feeling of sadness or lack of interest in activities that one once enjoyed. But depression is much more than simply feeling sad; it is a mental health condition that affects multiple aspects of life. People with depression often experience a profound lack of motivation and energy, and they may struggle with a variety of physical symptoms, including changes in sleep, appetite, and energy levels. Depression can also impact cognitive functioning, making it harder to concentrate, make decisions, and remember details.

Depression is often marked by two or more weeks of symptoms that interfere with an individual's ability to function in their personal, social, or professional lives. For some, depression may last for a relatively short period. For others, it can become a chronic issue, requiring long-term management and support. Depression is not a sign of weakness or a character flaw; it is a legitimate medical condition that can be treated and managed with the right approaches.

Types of Depression

Depression does not affect everyone in the same way. While some people may experience intense episodes that last for a few months, others may live with a low-grade, persistent form of depression for many years. Recognizing the different types of depression can help people better understand their own experiences and seek appropriate treatment.

1. Major Depressive Disorder (MDD)

Major Depressive Disorder, commonly known as MDD, is the most well-known form of depression. It is characterized by intense symptoms that last for a period of at least two weeks but often continue much longer. People with MDD may experience a combination of emotional, cognitive, and physical symptoms, including:

- Persistent sadness or feelings of emptiness

- Loss of interest in activities once enjoyed

- Changes in appetite or weight (either an increase or decrease)

- Difficulty sleeping (insomnia or sleeping too much)

- Feelings of worthlessness or excessive guilt

- Difficulty concentrating or making decisions

- Fatigue or low energy

- Thoughts of death or suicide

The hallmark of MDD is that it interferes significantly with daily life. People with MDD may find it difficult to get out of bed, go to work, or engage in social activities. It can be a debilitating condition, but treatments like therapy, medication, and lifestyle changes have been proven effective for many people.

2. Persistent Depressive Disorder (PDD)

Persistent Depressive Disorder, also known as dysthymia, is a milder but longer-lasting form of depression. Unlike MDD, which may appear in intense episodes, PDD involves a continuous low mood that lasts for at least two years. Symptoms of PDD are similar to those of MDD but are typically less severe. However, the chronic nature of PDD means that it can be just as disruptive as MDD, especially since it often goes untreated.

Symptoms of PDD can include:
- Low self-esteem
- Lack of energy
- Feelings of hopelessness
- Poor concentration or difficulty making decisions
- Loss of interest in daily activities

People with PDD often experience periods of more severe depressive symptoms, which may sometimes overlap with an episode of MDD—a condition known as "double depression." Although PDD symptoms are less intense, the ongoing, chronic nature of this disorder can make life feel persistently challenging.

3. Bipolar Disorder (formerly known as Manic Depression)

Bipolar Disorder is a mood disorder that includes episodes of depression as well as episodes of mania or hypomania (a less intense form of mania). During the depressive phases, individuals may experience symptoms similar to those found in MDD, including sadness, hopelessness, and fatigue. However, they also experience periods of elevated mood, high energy, and sometimes reckless behavior during the manic phases. Bipolar Disorder is further divided into:

- Bipolar I Disorder, which involves full manic episodes and, typically, depressive episodes.

- Bipolar II Disorder, which includes hypomanic episodes (a less severe form of mania) and depressive episodes.

Bipolar Disorder requires a different approach to treatment than unipolar depression because both the manic and depressive symptoms need to be managed, often with a combination of medication and therapy.

4. Seasonal Affective Disorder (SAD)

Seasonal Affective Disorder is a type of depression that follows a seasonal pattern, typically occurring during the fall and winter months when daylight hours are shorter. The lack of sunlight is thought to influence the brain's production of melatonin and serotonin, chemicals that help regulate mood. Common symptoms of SAD include:

- Increased sleep

- Low energy levels

- Weight gain or increased appetite

- Social withdrawal

SAD can have a significant impact on quality of life during the darker months, but many people find relief through light therapy (exposure to artificial sunlight), along with lifestyle changes, and sometimes medication.

5. Postpartum Depression

Postpartum Depression occurs in some women after giving birth and is believed to be linked to the hormonal changes that follow pregnancy, along with the stress of adapting to a new life with a baby. Unlike the "baby blues" that many mothers experience, postpartum depression is more intense and long-lasting, affecting the mother's ability to care for herself and her child. Symptoms include:

- Extreme sadness or despair
- Difficulty bonding with the baby
- Feelings of inadequacy as a mother
- Fear of harming oneself or the baby

This condition can be particularly challenging because of the stigma associated with experiencing negative emotions during a time society expects to be joyful. Postpartum Depression is treatable, and early intervention is essential for the well-being of both the mother and child.

6. Psychotic Depression

Psychotic Depression is a severe form of depression accompanied by psychotic symptoms such as hallucinations or delusions. These symptoms may be related to feelings of worthlessness or failure, and the person may become detached from reality. Psychotic Depression is very serious and requires immediate medical attention. Treatment usually involves a combination of antidepressants and antipsychotic medications, as well as therapy.

7. Premenstrual Dysphoric Disorder (PMDD)

PMDD is a severe form of premenstrual syndrome (PMS) that occurs in the weeks before menstruation and includes symptoms of depression, irritability, and anxiety. PMDD is thought to be triggered by hormonal fluctuations and can have a significant impact on daily functioning. Treatment options may include lifestyle adjustments, medication, and sometimes hormonal therapy.

8. Situational Depression

Situational Depression, also known as adjustment disorder with depressed mood, is triggered by a specific life event, such as the loss of a loved one, job loss, or a major life change. Symptoms are similar to those of major depression but are generally less severe and often improve as the person adapts to the change. Situational Depression can be a normal response to life's challenges, but support from friends, family, and therapy can help individuals move through it more quickly.

The Importance of Recognizing Different Types of Depression

Understanding the different types of depression is crucial, as each type requires a slightly different approach to treatment. What works for one person may not be effective for another, and knowing the specific nature of one's depression can be a step toward a more tailored, effective approach to managing it.

Moving Forward with Compassion and Understanding

Depression, in all its forms, can feel overwhelming and isolating. Yet, it's important to remember that it is also a highly treatable condition. By understanding the unique characteristics of each type of depression, individuals can take the first step toward managing their symptoms in a way that is compassionate and effective.

Symptoms and Causes of Depression

Depression is a complex mental health condition with a wide range of symptoms that affect each individual differently. While some symptoms of depression are well-known, others can be subtle or masked by other aspects of behavior and personality. Depression can also have multiple causes, from biological and psychological factors to social and spiritual influences. Understanding both the symptoms and causes is an essential first step to managing and overcoming depression.

Recognizing Symptoms of Depression

Depression doesn't look the same for everyone. It varies in intensity, duration, and manifestation, meaning that two people may experience vastly different symptoms and still share the diagnosis of depression. Some symptoms are common and widely recognized, while others can be less obvious or even hidden.

Common Symptoms of Depression

1. Persistent Sadness or Low Mood: One of the most recognizable signs of depression is a continuous feeling of sadness or emptiness that does not easily go away. This sadness may linger for weeks, months, or even years.

2. Loss of Interest or Pleasure in Activities: Known as anhedonia, this symptom refers to a lack of interest in hobbies, work, relationships, and other activities that were once enjoyable. Life may feel "flat" or meaningless, leading to social withdrawal and isolation.

3. Changes in Appetite or Weight: Depression can disrupt appetite, leading to significant weight loss or weight gain. Some people may eat too little, finding that food has lost its appeal, while others may eat more than usual as a way of coping.

4. Sleep Disturbances: Sleep issues are common in people with depression, whether it's insomnia (difficulty falling or staying asleep), hypersomnia (excessive sleep), or non-restorative sleep (waking up feeling unrefreshed).

5. Fatigue or Low Energy: Depression can leave individuals feeling physically and mentally exhausted, even after a full night's sleep. This fatigue often makes even simple daily tasks feel overwhelming.

6. Feelings of Worthlessness or Excessive Guilt: People with depression may struggle with feelings of inadequacy, self-blame, or guilt, often unrelated to actual events or circumstances.

7. Difficulty Concentrating or Making Decisions: Depression can impair cognitive functions, making it hard to focus, remember information, or make decisions. This often affects work, school, and personal responsibilities.

8. Thoughts of Death or Suicide: In severe cases, depression can lead to thoughts of death or suicide. It's essential to take these thoughts seriously and seek help immediately.

Less Obvious Symptoms of Depression

1. Physical Pain: Depression can manifest physically, with symptoms such as headaches, muscle aches, or back pain that have no clear medical cause. This is because depression affects the brain's regulation of pain perception.

2. Irritability and Restlessness: For some, depression shows up as frustration, anger, or irritability, often directed at themselves or those around them. This can be particularly prevalent in younger individuals and men.

3. Social Withdrawal and Isolation: Depression can make social interactions feel exhausting or pointless, leading to withdrawal from family, friends, and social activities.

4. Indecisiveness and Procrastination: People with depression often struggle to make decisions, even about small things. This can result in delays, procrastination, and avoidance of tasks.

5. Loss of Motivation and Purpose: Depression may strip individuals of their sense of purpose or meaning in life. Daily activities may feel pointless, and aspirations or future goals can seem unattainable.

6. Unexplained Anxiety: Although anxiety and depression are distinct conditions, they often overlap. People with depression may experience feelings of unease, worry, or panic without an obvious cause.

7. Negative or Pessimistic Thinking Patterns: Depression often creates a mental "filter" through which individuals view themselves, others, and the world in a negative or pessimistic way.

Exploring the Causes of Depression

Understanding the causes of depression is challenging, as they vary greatly from person to person. Research suggests that depression is often the result of a combination of biological, psychological, social, and spiritual factors. These factors interact in complex ways, making each person's experience of depression unique.

Biological Causes

1. Genetics: Research has shown that depression can run in families, suggesting a genetic component. If a person has a close relative with depression, they are at a higher risk of developing the condition themselves. However, genetics alone do not determine whether someone will experience depression; environmental and psychological factors also play significant roles.

2. Brain Chemistry and Function: Depression is often associated with imbalances in neurotransmitters—chemicals in the brain that regulate mood and emotion, such as serotonin, dopamine, and norepinephrine. Low levels of these neurotransmitters can lead to depressive symptoms, though it is still unclear whether these chemical imbalances are a cause or effect of depression.

3. Hormones: Hormonal changes can trigger or worsen depression, especially in certain stages of life. For example, women may be more vulnerable to depression

during pregnancy, postpartum, and menopause, while men may experience hormonal-related depression later in life.

4. Medical Conditions: Certain medical conditions, such as chronic illness, pain, and thyroid disorders, are linked to an increased risk of depression. Chronic conditions can affect physical health and mood, creating a cycle that makes managing depression more difficult.

Psychological Causes

1. Personality Traits: People with certain personality traits may be more susceptible to depression. Perfectionism, low self-esteem, excessive self-criticism, and a tendency to overthink are all traits that can contribute to depressive thinking patterns.

2. Negative Thinking Patterns: Individuals who tend to view themselves, others, and the world in a pessimistic or critical way are at a higher risk for depression. This includes cognitive distortions like catastrophizing (expecting the worst), black-and-white thinking, and overgeneralizing.

3. Stress and Trauma: Trauma, especially in childhood, can increase the risk of depression later in life. Experiences such as abuse, neglect, or losing a parent can create lasting emotional wounds. High-stress events, like job loss, divorce, or the death of a loved one, can also trigger or exacerbate depression.

4. Poor Coping Mechanisms: Individuals who struggle with unhealthy coping mechanisms, such as avoidance, denial, or substance abuse, may find it harder to manage depressive symptoms effectively.

Social Causes

1. Isolation and Loneliness: Social connections are essential for emotional well-being, and a lack of meaningful relationships can contribute to depression. Feelings of isolation or social exclusion can lead to a sense of purposelessness and exacerbate depressive symptoms.

2. Family Environment: Growing up in an environment where mental health issues are stigmatized, minimized, or ignored can increase the likelihood of depression. Family dynamics, such as conflict or lack of support, can also play a significant role.

3. Economic and Occupational Stress: Financial instability, job loss, and career-related stress are significant risk factors for depression. Economic hardship can lead to feelings of inadequacy and hopelessness, while job stress can create burnout and emotional exhaustion.

4. Social Media and Cultural Pressures: The prevalence of social media can intensify feelings of inadequacy and self-doubt, as individuals often compare themselves to others. Cultural and societal expectations can add further stress, influencing how people perceive their worth and success.

Spiritual Causes

1. Loss of Meaning or Purpose: A spiritual void, where an individual lacks a sense of purpose or connection to something greater than themselves, can contribute to depression. People who experience a loss of faith, doubt their beliefs, or feel disconnected from their values may find themselves struggling with depression.

2. Unresolved Guilt or Shame: Spiritual beliefs sometimes involve a moral or ethical framework, and when people feel they've failed to live up to these standards, they may experience guilt or shame. This unresolved guilt can weigh heavily on the mind, leading to depressive symptoms.

3. Existential Questions: For some, depression is linked to existential or spiritual questions—questions about life's meaning, purpose, and value. Wrestling with these issues can lead to a crisis of faith, creating a sense of emptiness or despair.

4. Community and Belonging: A lack of connection to a faith community or spiritual support network can lead to feelings of isolation, especially in difficult times. Those without a supportive community may find it harder to navigate life's challenges and sustain their mental health.

The Interplay of Multiple Factors

Depression is rarely caused by a single factor. Rather, it often results from a combination of biological vulnerabilities, psychological patterns, social circumstances, and spiritual concerns. For example, a person with a family history of depression may be more susceptible, but stress at work or a crisis of faith might be the triggering factors. Alternatively, someone with strong coping mechanisms and social support may be less affected by genetic predispositions. Recognizing this complex interplay can guide a more comprehensive approach to treatment, considering all aspects of a person's life and circumstances.

Understanding the various symptoms and causes of depression provides a foundation for developing a personalized, holistic approach to recovery. Depression is a challenging and often persistent condition, but with knowledge, support, and effective tools, it is manageable. This journey involves exploring every facet of one's life—physical, mental, social, and spiritual—to foster healing and resilience.

Psychological Theories on Depression

Understanding depression through psychological theories helps shed light on why people experience depression and how various treatment approaches address its symptoms. The three primary theories—cognitive, behavioral, and psychoanalytic—offer distinct perspectives on the causes and mechanisms behind depression. Each theory highlights specific elements that contribute to depressive feelings and behaviors, providing insights that are foundational for therapeutic approaches.

Cognitive Theories of Depression

Cognitive theories of depression emphasize the role of thought patterns and belief systems in contributing to depressive symptoms. These theories suggest that depression is closely tied to negative thought patterns, or cognitive distortions, that shape how individuals perceive themselves, others, and the world.

Aaron Beck's Cognitive Theory

Aaron Beck's cognitive theory is one of the most influential approaches in understanding depression. Beck proposed that people with depression often develop a "negative cognitive triad," which consists of:

1. Negative views about the self: Depressed individuals may believe they are inadequate, unworthy, or flawed. This belief can lead to feelings of self-loathing or guilt.

2. Negative views about the world: They may perceive the world as unfair, hostile, or overly demanding. This can make daily life feel overwhelming and foster a sense of hopelessness.

3. Negative views about the future: People with depression might believe that their situation will never improve. This sense of despair often underlies thoughts of giving up or withdrawing from life.

Beck identified several common cognitive distortions that are often present in depression:

- Catastrophizing: Assuming the worst-case scenario will happen.

- Overgeneralization: Drawing broad conclusions based on a single event.

- All-or-nothing thinking: Viewing situations in black-and-white terms without acknowledging shades of gray.

- Personalization: Blaming oneself for things that are outside of personal control.

- Selective abstraction: Focusing on a single negative detail and ignoring positive aspects of an experience.

Beck's cognitive therapy, now widely known as cognitive-behavioral therapy (CBT), aims to help individuals recognize and change these distorted thought patterns. By challenging negative beliefs and learning healthier thinking habits, individuals can reduce depressive symptoms and improve their mood.

Albert Ellis's Rational Emotive Behavior Therapy (REBT)

Albert Ellis developed Rational Emotive Behavior Therapy, another cognitive approach that highlights the impact of irrational beliefs on emotional well-being. Ellis argued that people often hold rigid and unrealistic expectations of themselves, others, and the world, leading to emotional distress. In REBT, these beliefs are commonly categorized as:

- Musturbatory thinking: Holding beliefs that things "must" be a certain way, such as "I must be perfect" or "Others must treat me fairly."

- Awfulizing: Believing that if things don't go as desired, it would be a complete catastrophe.

- Low frustration tolerance: Feeling incapable of handling setbacks or disappointments.

REBT focuses on helping individuals identify these irrational beliefs and replace them with more flexible, realistic perspectives. This approach empowers individuals to respond to challenging situations without succumbing to depressive thoughts.

Behavioral Theories of Depression

Behavioral theories focus on the idea that depression is a learned response to one's environment and that it results from a lack of positive reinforcement or a surplus of negative reinforcement. In this view, depression is maintained by patterns of behavior that reinforce feelings of sadness, hopelessness, and inactivity.

Lewinsohn's Behavioral Model

Peter Lewinsohn's behavioral model of depression posits that depression results from a lack of positive reinforcement. According to this theory, when people experience a reduction in enjoyable or rewarding activities, they are likely to feel more depressed. This lack of positive reinforcement might stem from:

- Environmental factors: Losing a job, ending a relationship, or experiencing isolation can reduce access to rewarding activities or social interactions.

- Skill deficits: Individuals who struggle with social skills may find it challenging to build relationships or seek support, leading to fewer positive experiences.

- Negative reinforcement: Sometimes, depressive behaviors (such as withdrawing from activities or expressing sadness) are inadvertently reinforced by others who provide sympathy or attention.

Lewinsohn's model emphasizes the importance of increasing positive activities and social interactions to break the cycle of depression. Behavioral activation, a treatment technique rooted in this theory, encourages individuals to gradually engage in activities that are enjoyable or fulfilling, helping them reconnect with sources of positive reinforcement.

Learned Helplessness Theory

The learned helplessness theory, developed by Martin Seligman, suggests that depression arises when people feel they have no control over their circumstances. Based on studies with animals, Seligman observed that individuals who experience repeated failures or negative events may come to believe that nothing they do will change their situation. This sense of helplessness can lead to:

- Reduced motivation: People who feel helpless may stop trying to improve their situation, believing that any effort would be pointless.

- Low self-esteem: Persistent feelings of helplessness can erode self-confidence, making individuals feel incapable or inadequate.

- Negative emotional response: This belief often results in feelings of sadness, apathy, and despair.

Learned helplessness theory provides the foundation for interventions that help individuals recognize and regain a sense of control. By setting small, achievable goals and building on successes, people can rebuild their confidence and reduce feelings of helplessness.

Psychoanalytic Theories of Depression

Psychoanalytic theories, rooted in the work of Sigmund Freud, focus on unconscious processes, unresolved conflicts, and early life experiences as key contributors to depression. These theories view depression as originating from internalized emotions or unresolved feelings related to loss and guilt.

Freud's Mourning and Melancholia

In his essay "Mourning and Melancholia," Freud proposed that depression (or "melancholia") shares certain characteristics with grief but is distinct in its intensity and origin. Freud suggested that individuals who experience depression may have unresolved grief or anger that has been turned inward. According to Freud:

- Loss: Depression is often triggered by some form of loss, which could be the loss of a loved one, a job, a status, or even a part of one's identity.

- Internalized anger: When individuals cannot openly express their anger, they may turn it inward, leading to feelings of guilt and self-reproach.

- Unconscious conflicts: Depression may stem from unresolved unconscious conflicts, often originating from childhood experiences or complex family dynamics.

Freudian psychoanalytic therapy aims to bring these unconscious feelings and conflicts to the surface, allowing individuals to process and resolve them. By addressing these underlying issues, individuals can release repressed emotions and work toward psychological healing.

Object Relations Theory

Object relations theory, developed by psychoanalysts such as Melanie Klein and Donald Winnicott, focuses on the impact of early relationships, particularly with caregivers, on the development of depression. According to this theory:

- Early attachments: The quality of a person's early relationships influences their capacity for emotional regulation and self-worth. Individuals who experience inconsistent or neglectful caregiving may struggle to form healthy attachments, increasing vulnerability to depression.

- Internalized "objects": People form mental representations of their caregivers, known as "objects." If these objects are associated with negative feelings, such as fear or abandonment, they may develop a negative self-image and struggle with depressive feelings.

Fear of abandonment: Depression can also stem from a fear of being abandoned or rejected. This fear may cause individuals to isolate themselves, thereby reinforcing their loneliness and sadness.

In therapeutic settings, object relations therapy helps individuals explore their early relationships, understand how these relationships have influenced their self-image, and develop healthier attachment patterns.

Integrating Cognitive, Behavioral, and Psychoanalytic Perspectives

While cognitive, behavioral, and psychoanalytic theories approach depression from different angles, they each offer valuable insights. Cognitive theories highlight the importance of thought patterns, behavioral theories focus on the role of environmental reinforcements, and psychoanalytic theories emphasize the impact of unconscious conflicts and early relationships. By integrating these perspectives, therapists can offer a holistic approach to treatment, addressing the complex nature of depression from multiple viewpoints.

In later chapters, this book will explore how these theories guide various treatment methods, from cognitive-behavioral therapy and behavioral activation to psychoanalytic and attachment-based therapies. Each approach has strengths, and combining them allows for a comprehensive treatment plan that considers the full scope of depression's causes and symptoms.

Depression, as a multifaceted condition, requires understanding and intervention on multiple levels. These theories form the foundation of many therapeutic techniques, each offering individuals a path toward recovery and resilience. The journey of managing depression is personal, but with the knowledge and tools derived from these psychological perspectives, it's a journey that can lead to healing and growth.

Theological Insights into Suffering and Healing

Depression and emotional suffering can feel overwhelming, and many seek solace in their faith, looking to divine wisdom for answers and comfort. The Bible offers rich insights into suffering and hope, presenting stories, teachings, and prophecies that speak to the heart of those experiencing deep emotional pain. This chapter explores the Bible's teachings on suffering, healing, and divine intervention, offering a theological framework for understanding mental health struggles and finding comfort in God's presence.

Biblical Perspectives on Suffering

The Bible does not shy away from the reality of suffering. Throughout both the Old and New Testaments, we find stories of individuals who experienced pain, loss, grief, and despair, yet found strength and resilience through their faith. Understanding these biblical teachings on suffering can help us comprehend depression as part of the human experience while showing us how God offers hope even in the darkest moments.

Suffering as Part of the Human Condition

The Book of Job provides one of the Bible's most profound explorations of suffering. Job, a righteous man, endures immense physical and emotional pain after losing his wealth, health, and family. Despite his faithfulness, Job's suffering challenges his understanding of God's justice and compassion. His story highlights the mystery of suffering, showing that even those who follow God are not immune to trials. In Job 2:10, after losing everything, Job asks, "Shall we accept good from God, and not trouble?" (NIV). This verse points to a foundational truth: suffering is often part of our journey, and it does not necessarily reflect a lack of faith or divine displeasure.

Another key passage that speaks to the universal nature of suffering is found in Romans 5:3-4: "We also glory in our sufferings, because we know that suffering produces perseverance; perseverance, character; and character, hope." Paul's words underscore that suffering can shape and strengthen us, building character and hope within our hearts. This perspective provides comfort, reminding us that God can work through our pain, using it as a tool for personal and spiritual growth.

The Nature of Spiritual Warfare

The Bible also portrays suffering, including emotional suffering, as an aspect of spiritual warfare. In Ephesians 6:12, Paul writes, "For we wrestle not against flesh and blood, but against principalities, against powers, against the rulers of the darkness of this world, against spiritual wickedness in high places." This verse implies that our struggles may sometimes have spiritual dimensions. Depression and despair may feel amplified by forces that seek to undermine faith and hope. Recognizing this spiritual aspect can help believers turn to God's strength and armor, as Paul advises in Ephesians 6:13-18, to resist these forces and find resilience.

Finding Purpose in Suffering

The Bible often emphasizes that suffering, while difficult, can lead to spiritual growth and deepen one's relationship with God. In 2 Corinthians 1:3-4, Paul describes God as the "Father of compassion and the God of all comfort, who comforts us in all our troubles, so that we can comfort those in any trouble with the comfort we ourselves receive from God." Here, Paul points out that suffering can cultivate empathy and equip believers to support others. This purpose can infuse a sense of meaning into the pain, reframing it as an opportunity to serve and comfort others who experience similar struggles.

Hope and Healing in the Bible

While the Bible acknowledges suffering, it also offers hope and pathways toward healing. Scriptures reveal God's compassionate nature, showing that He is present in our pain and desires to bring us restoration. This hope is foundational for those battling depression, as it provides assurance that God is not indifferent to their struggles.

God's Presence in Times of Trouble

Psalm 34:18 offers comforting words to those in despair: "The Lord is close to the brokenhearted and saves those who are crushed in spirit." This verse reminds believers that God draws near to those in pain, offering comfort and solace. Similarly, in Psalm 147:3, we read, "He heals the brokenhearted and binds up their wounds." These verses highlight God's compassion and His desire to mend broken spirits, assuring those who are suffering that they are not alone.

Jesus as the Healer

The New Testament portrays Jesus as a healer, not only of physical ailments but also of emotional and spiritual wounds. In Matthew 11:28-30, Jesus invites those who are burdened to find rest in Him: "Come to me, all you who are weary and burdened, and I will give you rest. Take my yoke upon you and learn from me, for I am gentle and humble in heart, and you will find rest for your souls." This passage reveals Jesus' deep compassion and His desire to ease the suffering of those who seek Him. For those dealing with depression, Jesus' invitation can offer immense comfort and reassurance, providing a spiritual foundation upon which they can find peace.

The Power of Faith and Prayer

James 5:13-15 speaks to the importance of prayer in times of suffering: "Is anyone among you in trouble? Let them pray. Is anyone happy? Let them sing songs of praise." This passage encourages believers to turn to prayer when faced with difficulties. Prayer is not only a way to seek divine help; it also connects individuals with God, offering solace and a sense of hope.

The practice of prayer can be particularly healing for those with depression. Studies show that prayer and meditation can reduce stress, enhance emotional well-being, and increase resilience in times of adversity. In times of deep despair, prayer allows individuals to lay their burdens before God, fostering a sense of peace and strength.

Divine Intervention in Mental Health Struggles

Faith in divine intervention is a cornerstone of biblical teaching on healing. While psychological theories and therapeutic methods are valuable, theological perspectives affirm that God can work miraculously to bring healing and transformation.

Stories of Divine Healing

The Gospels are filled with accounts of Jesus healing individuals, both physically and emotionally. In Mark 5:1-20, Jesus encounters a man suffering from intense mental anguish and inner torment. After Jesus drives out the demons that plague him, the man is described as being "in his right mind" (Mark 5:15). This story illustrates Jesus' authority over all forms of suffering and His power to restore wholeness. Believers can draw strength from these accounts, seeing them as evidence that God desires to bring healing to every area of life.

Faith and Healing

Faith plays a crucial role in receiving God's healing. In Mark 5:34, Jesus tells a woman who had suffered for years, "Daughter, your faith has healed you. Go in peace and be freed from your suffering." Faith is not merely a passive state; it is an active trust in God's power and love. For those with depression, maintaining faith in God's ability to heal—even when circumstances feel bleak—can serve as a source of hope and strength.

However, it's important to note that faith-based healing does not always mean an instant cure. In 2 Corinthians 12:7-9, Paul describes a "thorn in the flesh" that he struggled with, despite praying for its removal. God's response to Paul was, "My grace is sufficient for you, for my power is made perfect in weakness." This passage reminds believers that healing may come in different forms, sometimes as a journey of resilience and strength rather than immediate relief.

Integrating Faith with Psychological Treatment

The Bible's teachings on suffering and healing can be integrated with psychological treatments to provide a holistic approach to mental health. Faith and psychological interventions are not mutually exclusive; rather, they can complement each other, addressing both the spiritual and emotional aspects of depression.

The Role of Community and Support

Galatians 6:2 encourages believers to "carry each other's burdens, and in this way you will fulfill the law of Christ." Community and fellowship are integral to healing, as they provide support, encouragement, and accountability. Churches and faith-based support groups can offer a nurturing environment where individuals feel understood and uplifted. This support system, coupled with professional care, can make a significant difference in managing depression.

Embracing God's Grace and Compassion

Finally, theological perspectives remind us of God's boundless grace and compassion. In Psalm 103:13-14, we read, "As a father has compassion on his children, so the Lord has compassion on those who fear him; for he knows how we are formed, he remembers that we are dust." God's understanding of our weaknesses provides comfort, especially during times of emotional struggle. Embracing God's grace allows individuals to release self-condemnation and find hope and acceptance in His love.

This chapter has explored the Bible's insights into suffering and healing, revealing a compassionate God who is intimately aware of human pain. Theological perspectives on suffering and hope provide solace and strength, offering a foundation for those struggling with depression. By integrating biblical wisdom with psychological treatments, individuals can find holistic healing, supported by both faith and therapy. Depression, though a challenging journey, can become a path to deeper faith, resilience, and closeness with God.

CHAPTER 02

THE ROLE OF EXERCISE IN MENTAL HEALTH

Exercise has long been recognized for its benefits on physical health, but its positive impact on mental health is equally profound. For individuals battling depression or anxiety, physical activity can serve as a powerful tool in managing symptoms, improving mood, and reducing stress. This chapter explores the mechanisms through which exercise benefits mental health, the types of exercise best suited for improving mood, and how to incorporate physical activity into a daily routine for maximum benefit.

How Exercise Helps: The Science Behind It

Regular physical activity influences the brain in ways that can reduce symptoms of depression and anxiety. These benefits are largely due to chemical changes that occur in the brain when we exercise, as well as the impact exercise has on our body's stress response and overall well-being.

Endorphin Release: Nature's Mood Lifters

One of the most immediate effects of exercise on the brain is the release of endorphins, often called "feel-good" hormones. Endorphins are neurotransmitters that relieve pain and induce a sense of pleasure or euphoria. When we engage in physical activity, especially at moderate to high intensities, the brain releases higher levels of endorphins. This is sometimes called the "runner's high," a phenomenon where people feel an elevated mood, reduced anxiety, and a temporary relief from pain after exercise.

Endorphins not only create a positive mood state but also help combat the persistent low energy and motivation often associated with depression. By increasing endorphin levels, exercise can provide a natural "boost" that elevates energy levels and enhances emotional well-being.

Reduction of Stress Hormones

In addition to increasing endorphin levels, exercise helps regulate stress hormones like cortisol. Cortisol is essential for the body's response to stress, but when it remains elevated due to chronic stress or mental health issues, it can negatively affect mood, immune function, and physical health. High cortisol levels are commonly associated with feelings of anxiety, irritability, and depression.

Exercise, particularly aerobic activities like running, swimming, or brisk walking, helps reduce cortisol levels in the body, leading to a greater sense of calm and balance. The physical act of exercise also triggers the parasympathetic nervous system, which counteracts the body's stress response and induces relaxation. This dual effect of reducing cortisol and activating the body's relaxation response can be incredibly helpful for managing depression and stress.

Enhancing Neuroplasticity

Research indicates that regular physical activity can improve neuroplasticity, which is the brain's ability to adapt and reorganize itself by forming new neural connections. Depression has been linked to decreased neuroplasticity, particularly in regions like the hippocampus, which plays a crucial role in mood regulation and memory.

Exercise stimulates the production of brain-derived neurotrophic factor (BDNF), a protein that supports the growth and maintenance of neurons. BDNF promotes neurogenesis (the growth of new neurons) and enhances synaptic connections, improving cognitive functions and emotional resilience. As BDNF levels increase with regular physical activity, it strengthens the brain's ability to cope with stress and fosters a greater sense of mental stability.

Boosting Serotonin and Dopamine Levels

Serotonin and dopamine are neurotransmitters involved in mood regulation, motivation, and reward. Low levels of serotonin are commonly associated with depression, while a dopamine imbalance can affect motivation and pleasure. Exercise can help balance serotonin and dopamine levels, particularly with consistent, moderate-intensity activities like walking, cycling, or strength training.

Exercise increases the availability of tryptophan, a precursor to serotonin, which leads to higher serotonin production in the brain. Additionally, physical activity activates dopamine pathways, which is particularly important for people experiencing anhedonia (a common symptom of depression where one feels little to no pleasure in activities). By stabilizing serotonin and dopamine levels, exercise can enhance mood, motivation, and overall life satisfaction.

Types of Exercise Beneficial for Mental Health

While any form of exercise can positively impact mental health, certain types have been shown to be particularly effective for alleviating symptoms of depression and anxiety. The key is finding activities that are enjoyable and sustainable, as consistency is vital for maximizing the mental health benefits of exercise.

Aerobic Exercise

Aerobic exercises, such as jogging, cycling, swimming, and brisk walking, are some of the most beneficial forms of physical activity for mental health. Aerobic exercise increases heart rate, enhances circulation, and triggers the release of endorphins and neurotransmitters associated with mood improvement. Studies consistently show that moderate-intensity aerobic exercise can reduce depressive symptoms and improve anxiety, often with effects comparable to those of antidepressant medications.

For individuals who are new to exercise, starting with a simple daily walk can have profound benefits. Walking outdoors has the added advantage of exposing the individual to natural sunlight, which can further elevate mood by boosting vitamin D levels and regulating circadian rhythms.

Resistance Training

Resistance or strength training, which includes exercises such as weight lifting, bodyweight exercises, or resistance band workouts, also positively impacts mental health. Engaging in resistance training helps increase muscle strength, builds self-confidence, and can provide a sense of achievement and empowerment. This type of exercise can improve mood and reduce symptoms of depression and anxiety.

Research suggests that low-to-moderate intensity resistance training is particularly effective for improving mental health, especially when done consistently (about two to three times per week). Strength training's effect on body image and self-esteem can also be valuable for those struggling with self-worth as a result of depression.

Mind-Body Exercises

Mind-body exercises, like yoga, tai chi, and Pilates, combine physical movement with mindful awareness and breath control. These activities are particularly beneficial for managing stress and anxiety, as they incorporate techniques that help regulate the body's stress response.

Yoga, in particular, has been studied extensively for its impact on mental health. Practicing yoga encourages deep breathing, mindfulness, and relaxation, which help reduce cortisol levels, alleviate anxiety, and promote a sense of inner peace. For people experiencing depression, yoga can offer a means of connecting mind and body, fostering self-compassion, and grounding oneself in the present moment.

Building Exercise into Daily Life

Starting and maintaining an exercise routine can be challenging, especially for those dealing with depression. However, incorporating physical activity into daily life can be achieved by taking small, manageable steps. Here are some strategies to help integrate exercise into a routine in ways that are sustainable and enjoyable.

Start Small and Set Realistic Goals

For many, the thought of an intense workout can be intimidating, especially when dealing with low motivation. Instead of aiming for a high level of activity immediately, begin with small steps—such as a 10-minute walk or a few gentle stretches. Setting achievable goals creates a sense of accomplishment, which can build momentum and motivation over time. Gradually increasing the duration or intensity of activity can prevent burnout and make exercise feel more manageable.

Find Activities You Enjoy

The best exercise is the one you'll do consistently, and enjoyment plays a major role in adherence. Trying different activities—such as dancing, swimming, hiking, or joining a sports league—can help in finding what feels enjoyable and engaging. Many people find that when they focus on activities they genuinely like, exercise becomes something they look forward to rather than a chore.

Incorporate Social Interaction

Exercising with others can boost motivation and add a social dimension to physical activity. Group classes, walking with friends, or joining a community sports team can make exercise more enjoyable while providing social support. For those who feel isolated due to depression, this connection with others can be an important factor in improving mood and reducing feelings of loneliness.

Use Exercise as a Form of Self-Care

Viewing exercise as a form of self-care can shift one's perspective, making it easier to prioritize. Instead of seeing exercise as another task to check off, it can be reframed as an act of kindness toward oneself. Taking time to move the body and relieve stress is a way to nurture mental and emotional health.

Incorporate Mindfulness into Exercise

Adding mindfulness to physical activity can enhance its mental health benefits. Being present during exercise—paying attention to breathing, the sensations in the body, or the sounds and sights in the surroundings—can create a more fulfilling experience. This approach, often called "mindful movement," reduces stress and brings an increased sense of relaxation and focus to the activity.

Exercise is a natural, effective, and accessible method for managing mental health symptoms, particularly those related to depression and anxiety. By understanding the scientific mechanisms behind exercise's impact on mood and incorporating enjoyable, achievable activities into daily life, individuals can build resilience, improve their emotional well-being, and find a sense of control over their mental health. Embracing physical activity as part of a holistic approach to wellness offers a pathway to healing, one step at a time.

Types of Beneficial Exercises for Mental Health

Exercise is a powerful tool for improving mental health, and while nearly any form of physical activity can offer benefits, certain types of exercise are particularly effective in promoting emotional and psychological well-being. In this chapter, we'll explore several forms of exercise—walking, yoga, swimming, strength training, and mindfulness-focused activities like tai chi—that have proven benefits for mental health. Each of these exercises offers unique advantages, so finding a type that aligns with one's interests and lifestyle can make it easier to stay consistent and fully experience the positive effects on mood and stress levels.

Walking: A Simple Path to Wellness

One of the easiest and most accessible forms of exercise, walking offers numerous mental health benefits. It requires no special equipment, can be done anywhere, and is gentle enough for people of all ages and fitness levels.

Benefits of Walking

1. Mood Improvement: Walking, especially in nature, has been shown to lift mood and increase feelings of calm and happiness. Studies indicate that as little as 30 minutes of moderate walking can reduce symptoms of depression and anxiety. Walking outdoors, particularly in green spaces or natural settings, amplifies these effects due to the calming influence of nature.

2. Stress Reduction: Walking encourages deep, rhythmic breathing, which activates the body's relaxation response and helps reduce levels of the stress hormone cortisol. Many people find that walking is an excellent way to clear their minds, providing a mental break from the stresses of daily life.

3. Boosting Energy and Motivation: For those experiencing low energy or motivation—a common symptom of depression—walking offers a manageable starting point. The physical activity releases endorphins, which create a natural energy boost and elevate mood.

Practical Tips for Getting Started with Walking

- Start Small: Begin with a manageable goal, such as a 10–15-minute walk each day. This can be gradually increased as comfort and motivation improve.

- Walk in Nature: When possible, try walking in parks or natural areas. Nature walks have added mental health benefits due to their relaxing and refreshing effects on the mind.

- Make it Social: Walking with a friend or a group can make the experience enjoyable and provide social support, which is also beneficial for mental health.

Yoga: Mind, Body, and Breath Connection

Yoga is a mind-body exercise that combines physical postures with mindful breathing and meditation. Originating in ancient India, yoga has become a popular practice worldwide, known for its holistic approach to wellness and stress relief.

Benefits of Yoga

1. Reduces Anxiety and Depression: Yoga's slow, controlled movements and deep breathing techniques can lower anxiety and depressive symptoms by stimulating the body's relaxation response and regulating the nervous system.

2. Enhances Self-Awareness and Mindfulness: Practicing yoga promotes mindfulness, encouraging individuals to stay present and focus on their breath and body sensations. This self-awareness can help people process emotions in a healthy way and reduce negative thought patterns.

3. Increases Resilience: By combining physical strength and flexibility training with mental focus, yoga helps build resilience, both physically and mentally. Over time, this can enhance one's ability to cope with stress and adversity.

Practical Tips for Getting Started with Yoga

- Choose the Right Style: Yoga has many styles, from gentle (such as Hatha or Yin) to more dynamic (like Vinyasa or Ashtanga). Beginners may prefer a gentle or restorative practice that focuses on stretching, breathing, and relaxation.

- Practice Regularly: Consistency is key. Aim for a few sessions each week, even if they're just 15–20 minutes long. Many online classes and apps offer beginner sessions that can be done at home.

- Focus on Breathwork: Breathing exercises (pranayama) are central to yoga. Learning to breathe deeply and slowly can help calm the mind, reduce stress, and improve focus.

Swimming: A Refreshing Full-Body Workout

Swimming is a full-body workout that provides physical and mental health benefits. The water's buoyancy reduces the impact on joints, making it an ideal exercise for people of all ages and fitness levels. Swimming can be both invigorating and meditative, depending on the style and pace.

Benefits of Swimming

1. Mood Enhancement: Swimming stimulates the release of endorphins and other neurotransmitters, helping to elevate mood and alleviate feelings of stress or sadness. Additionally, the rhythmic, repetitive motions of swimming can have a calming, meditative effect.

2. Relief from Anxiety: The sensation of water on the body can have a soothing effect, and swimming helps regulate breathing, which can ease anxiety. The buoyancy of water also provides a feeling of weightlessness, reducing physical tension.

3. Improved Sleep: For those struggling with insomnia or poor sleep due to anxiety or depression, swimming can improve sleep quality. Physical exertion, combined with the calming effects of water, helps the body relax and prepares it for restful sleep.

Practical Tips for Getting Started with Swimming

- Start Slowly: Begin with a few laps at a comfortable pace, gradually increasing the intensity and duration as fitness improves.

- Try Different Strokes: Varying strokes like freestyle, backstroke, or breaststroke can work different muscle groups and keep the routine interesting.

- Practice Consistency: Aim for two to three swimming sessions per week, which can help in maintaining physical fitness and mental well-being.

Strength Training: Building Confidence and Resilience

Strength training, also known as resistance training, involves exercises that build muscle strength and endurance through the use of weights, resistance bands, or body weight. Although it's typically associated with physical fitness, strength training also offers significant mental health benefits.

Benefits of Strength Training

1. Boosts Self-Esteem and Confidence: Seeing progress in physical strength over time can improve self-

esteem and confidence. For individuals with depression, this sense of accomplishment can be highly empowering.

2. Reduces Symptoms of Depression: Studies have shown that strength training can reduce symptoms of depression, likely due to its ability to regulate neurotransmitters and stress hormones. It also improves sleep quality and energy levels, both of which are often impaired in depression.

3. Provides a Focused, Goal-Oriented Activity: Strength training is often goal-driven, focusing on gradual progress in strength and endurance. This focus on incremental improvement can foster motivation and purpose, which are important in the recovery from depression.

Practical Tips for Getting Started with Strength Training

- Start Light: Begin with light weights or bodyweight exercises, focusing on proper form. Over time, gradually increase the weight or resistance.

- Create a Routine: Incorporate strength training into a weekly routine, with 2–3 sessions focused on different muscle groups.

- Track Progress: Keeping a record of progress can be motivating, showing tangible improvements in strength and endurance.

Tai Chi: The Art of Moving Meditation

Tai Chi, an ancient Chinese practice, is often described as "moving meditation." It involves slow, deliberate movements, deep breathing, and a focus on mindfulness. Although less intense than other forms of exercise, Tai Chi offers unique mental health benefits.

Benefits of Tai Chi

1. Reduces Stress and Anxiety: Tai Chi's slow, flowing movements encourage relaxation and help calm the mind. By focusing on gentle movement and breathing, it reduces stress and creates a meditative state that can relieve anxiety.

2. Improves Mindfulness and Concentration: Tai Chi requires attention to body position, balance, and breathing, which enhances mindfulness and helps center the mind. This focus on the present moment can reduce intrusive thoughts often associated with anxiety and depression.

3. Boosts Physical and Mental Resilience: Regular Tai Chi practice can improve physical balance, flexibility, and mental clarity. This increased resilience can help people better cope with stress and emotional challenges.

Practical Tips for Getting Started with Tai Chi

- Seek a Qualified Instructor: Tai Chi is best learned through direct instruction, as the movements require specific postures and breathing techniques.

- Practice Outdoors: Practicing Tai Chi outdoors, particularly in a natural setting, can enhance its calming effects.

- Focus on Consistency: Even short, daily Tai Chi sessions can offer significant mental health benefits, so consistency is key.

Finding What Works for You

Exercise is a flexible and powerful tool for mental health. Whether through the simplicity of walking, the mindfulness of yoga and Tai Chi, the refreshing qualities of swimming, or the confidence-building aspects of strength training, each type of exercise offers unique benefits. The key to reaping these benefits is consistency and choosing activities that you find enjoyable. By incorporating regular physical activity into your routine, you're investing in a practical, empowering, and sustainable way to improve mental health and enhance overall well-being.

Creating an Exercise Routine for Mental Health

Establishing a regular exercise routine can be one of the most transformative steps in managing mental health. However, for many people, especially those experiencing depression or anxiety, starting and sticking to a consistent exercise routine can be challenging. In this chapter, we'll explore practical, actionable steps to create a sustainable exercise routine, even on days when motivation and energy are low. By building consistency over time, exercise can become a reliable part of mental health care, offering benefits that range from mood improvement to stress reduction.

Understanding the Benefits of Routine

A structured exercise routine provides a sense of stability and predictability. Regular physical activity, performed consistently, can lead to physiological changes that positively impact mood, stress levels, and overall mental well-being. Beyond its immediate effects, a routine can reinforce positive behaviors, making it easier to stick with exercise long-term.

Step 1: Set Realistic, Achievable Goals

Setting realistic goals is the foundation of any successful exercise routine. For individuals experiencing mental health challenges, overly ambitious goals can be overwhelming. Instead, focus on small, manageable steps that gradually build confidence and stamina.

Examples of Realistic Goals

- Start Small: Begin with short sessions, such as a 10-minute walk or 5-minute stretching routine. The goal is simply to get moving, no matter how briefly, to create a habit.

- Focus on Consistency Over Intensity: Aim to exercise a certain number of times per week rather than focusing on intensity. For instance, committing to three short walks per week is an attainable goal that can help establish consistency.

- Set Incremental Goals: Once a basic routine is established, gradually increase the duration or intensity of the exercises. For example, extend a 10-minute walk to 15 minutes after a few weeks.

Step 2: Choose Enjoyable Activities

One of the biggest barriers to a consistent exercise routine is lack of enjoyment. Choose activities that feel enjoyable, engaging, or even relaxing. When exercise feels like a chore, it's difficult to maintain motivation, particularly on low-energy days.

Tips for Finding Enjoyable Activities

- Experiment with Different Types of Exercise: Try a variety of activities—walking, cycling, dancing, yoga, or even gardening—to see what feels most enjoyable.

- Incorporate Movement Into Daily Activities: Exercise doesn't have to be structured. Walking to a nearby store, dancing to music at home, or playing with a pet can all contribute to physical activity.

- Focus on Low-Intensity Options: On low-energy days, gentle activities like stretching, slow-paced yoga, or a calming walk can be both enjoyable and manageable.

Step 3: Create a Routine That Works for Your Lifestyle

A successful exercise routine fits seamlessly into one's lifestyle, rather than feeling like an additional burden. By identifying the best times for exercise and finding ways to integrate it into daily life, it becomes easier to stay consistent.

Building a Routine

- Find Your Ideal Time: Some people feel more energized in the morning, while others may prefer exercising in the afternoon or evening. Identify the time that feels most natural and energizing.

- Schedule Exercise Like an Appointment: Treat exercise as a non-negotiable part of the day. Mark it on your calendar or set a reminder to help make it a priority.

- Incorporate Exercise Into Everyday Activities: Simple actions like taking the stairs instead of the elevator, walking during lunch breaks, or stretching during TV commercials can help integrate movement into daily life.

Step 4: Make it Manageable on Low-Energy Days

Low-energy days are inevitable, especially for individuals experiencing depression, anxiety, or chronic stress. On these days, the thought of exercise may feel overwhelming. By adjusting expectations and creating a "low-energy" version of the routine, it's possible to maintain consistency without feeling pressure to perform at full intensity.

Tips for Low-Energy Days

- Scale Back: Allow yourself to do a less intense version of your usual routine. If a 20-minute walk feels like too much, try a 5-minute stroll instead. This keeps the habit alive without overwhelming yourself.

- Focus on Gentle, Restorative Activities: Gentle forms of exercise, such as stretching, breathing exercises, or a short yoga session, can be easier to manage on days when energy is low.

- Give Yourself Permission to Rest: Resting is part of self-care, too. If even a short, gentle activity feels too difficult, give yourself permission to rest without guilt. Focus on returning to your routine the next day or when you feel able.

Step 5: Track Progress and Celebrate Milestones

Tracking progress can be a powerful motivator. Seeing improvements over time reinforces the positive impact of exercise, helping to build self-esteem and resilience. This step is especially important for individuals managing depression, where feelings of low self-worth can interfere with motivation.

Ways to Track Progress

- Keep a Journal: Record each exercise session, noting how you feel before and after. This can help reveal patterns, such as the positive effects of exercise on mood.

- Celebrate Small Milestones: Small achievements—like completing a week of scheduled exercise or increasing walking time by five minutes—deserve celebration. Rewarding yourself reinforces the habit.

- Focus on Non-Physical Benefits: Track mental and emotional improvements, such as better sleep, lower stress levels, or improved mood. These benefits often appear before physical changes, reinforcing the value of the routine.

Step 6: Find Accountability and Support

Having accountability can make a significant difference, especially on days when motivation is low. Supportive friends, family members, or even an online community can provide encouragement, making it easier to stay on track.

Sources of Accountability

- Exercise with a Friend: Exercising with a friend or family member provides social interaction, which can boost mood, and adds accountability.

- Join a Class or Group: Exercise classes or groups provide a structured routine, making it easier to stay motivated. Many communities have free or low-cost walking groups, fitness classes, or online workout groups.

- Set Up a Rewards System: Establish small rewards for meeting exercise goals. This might be a favorite treat, a relaxing activity, or any reward that reinforces the effort you've made.

Step 7: Be Patient and Kind to Yourself

Building a new routine, especially one that impacts mental health, takes time. There may be setbacks, days when motivation wanes, or periods when life circumstances interfere with the routine. It's essential to treat yourself with patience and kindness, recognizing that every small effort contributes to long-term progress.

Tips for Self-Compassion

- Focus on Progress, Not Perfection: Small, consistent steps are more valuable than achieving perfection. It's normal for motivation to fluctuate; the key is to keep moving forward.

- Practice Positive Self-Talk: Replace self-critical thoughts with positive affirmations. Remind yourself that every effort counts and that you're building habits that support well-being.

- Reflect on Your Accomplishments: Periodically take time to reflect on the progress you've made. Celebrating your efforts, however small, helps reinforce the habit and builds confidence.

A Sample Routine for Mental Wellness

Creating a structured plan can help make exercise an automatic part of your day. Here's an example of a gentle, achievable weekly exercise routine designed to support mental health:

- Monday: 10-minute morning walk, focusing on deep breathing.

- Tuesday: 15 minutes of light yoga or stretching in the evening.

- Wednesday: Rest day with a 5-minute deep breathing or mindfulness practice.

- Thursday: 20-minute walk in nature or around the neighborhood.

- Friday: Strength training (light weights or bodyweight exercises) for 10 minutes.

- Saturday: Swimming, cycling, or a recreational activity for 15–20 minutes.

- Sunday: Reflective rest day with journaling or a 5-minute meditation.

Establishing a consistent exercise routine can be life-changing for mental health. By starting small, choosing enjoyable activities, and adapting the routine for low-energy days, it's possible to create a lasting habit that contributes to overall well-being. Remember, the journey is as important as the destination, and every small step taken is a step toward a healthier, more balanced life. Through patience, persistence, and self-compassion, anyone can develop a routine that nurtures both mind and body.

Theological Perspective: The Body as a Temple

The concept of the body as a temple is deeply rooted in biblical teachings, emphasizing that our physical bodies are more than mere vessels—they are sacred and valuable to God. By caring for our bodies, we not only honor our own well-being but also fulfill a spiritual calling. This chapter will explore how maintaining physical health is an act of worship and stewardship, one that aligns with the teachings of Scripture and can help support mental and spiritual well-being.

Understanding the Body as a Temple

The Apostle Paul speaks directly to the concept of the body as a temple in 1 Corinthians 6:19-20, stating:

> "Do you not know that your bodies are temples of the Holy Spirit, who is in you, whom you have received from God? You are not your own; you were bought at a price.

Therefore honor God with your bodies." (1 Corinthians 6:19-20, NIV)

In these verses, Paul emphasizes that our bodies are "temples" of the Holy Spirit. The Greek word used for "temple" (ναός, naos) implies a sacred, consecrated space. This understanding places a profound responsibility on each believer to respect and care for their body as a place where the divine dwells.

The Call to Stewardship

Stewardship is a fundamental biblical principle. God has given each person life, health, and physical existence, and it is our duty to manage these gifts wisely. This call to stewardship encompasses our bodies, which we are entrusted to care for and maintain. In Genesis, God creates humans in His image, endowing them with unique worth and purpose:

> "So God created mankind in his own image, in the image of God he created them; male and female he created them." (Genesis 1:27, NIV)

Being made in God's image implies a duty to respect that image by taking care of our bodies. This stewardship aligns with the call in Romans 12:1:

> "Therefore, I urge you, brothers and sisters, in view of God's mercy, to offer your bodies as a living sacrifice, holy

and pleasing to God—this is your true and proper worship." (Romans 12:1, NIV)

Here, Paul encourages believers to offer their bodies as a "living sacrifice," meaning that our physical well-being, actions, and choices can be expressions of worship to God. This act of devotion underscores that caring for our bodies is an essential part of a holistic spiritual life.

Health and Holiness

The concept of holiness often extends beyond the spiritual to include the physical, as evidenced in the dietary and health-related laws given to the Israelites in the Old Testament. While the specifics of these laws are distinct to Israel's covenant, they reveal God's desire for His people to live in health and holiness.

For example, in Leviticus 11, God provides dietary guidelines for His people to keep them physically healthy and spiritually pure. Although Christians are not bound by these dietary laws, the principle of living in a way that promotes health and holiness remains. By living in ways that honor the body, we fulfill God's desire for us to "be holy, because I am holy" (Leviticus 11:44).

Honoring God Through Physical Health

The importance of taking care of the body is further emphasized in the New Testament, where we see Jesus' ministry involving acts of physical healing. His healings were not only expressions of compassion but also reminders that physical health matters in God's kingdom. Jesus healed various ailments, showing that He cared deeply about the physical well-being of people.

The Connection Between Physical and Spiritual Health

The Bible reflects a holistic view of health, acknowledging that physical well-being is interconnected with spiritual and emotional well-being. Proverbs 3:7-8 highlights this relationship:

> "Do not be wise in your own eyes; fear the Lord and shun evil. This will bring health to your body and nourishment to your bones." (Proverbs 3:7-8, NIV)

This passage suggests that honoring God and following His ways have a tangible impact on one's physical health. In the same way, neglecting physical well-being can hinder our ability to serve and honor God. By maintaining a healthy lifestyle, we enhance our capacity to live out our purpose and engage fully in God's work.

Practical Ways to Honor God Through Our Bodies

1. Exercise as Worship: Engaging in regular physical activity can be viewed as an act of worship. Exercise strengthens the body, enhances mood, and provides mental clarity, allowing us to serve God more effectively. By

honoring our physical well-being, we prepare ourselves to better fulfill His purposes.

2. Healthy Eating as Stewardship: Consuming foods that nourish rather than harm our bodies is a form of stewardship. The Bible advocates for self-control and discipline, as reflected in 1 Corinthians 10:31:

> "So whether you eat or drink or whatever you do, do it all for the glory of God." (1 Corinthians 10:31, NIV)

By making mindful choices in our diet, we can honor God through our bodies, equipping ourselves to serve Him with vitality and strength.

3. Rest and Sabbath: Physical rest is essential for maintaining good health. The Bible prescribes rest, both through Sabbath observance and principles of balance and renewal. Jesus Himself took time to rest (Mark 6:31), teaching us that rest is not only permissible but necessary. Taking care of our bodies by resting honors God's design for us and refreshes us for His work.

4. Avoiding Harmful Substances: Scriptures also encourage us to avoid anything that could harm our bodies or hinder our spiritual walk. For instance, Proverbs 20:1 warns:

> "Wine is a mocker and beer a brawler; whoever is led astray by them is not wise." (Proverbs 20:1, NIV)

While this verse specifically addresses alcohol, the principle extends to anything that may compromise our health, mental clarity, or ability to honor God fully.

Embracing the Body as a Sacred Vessel

Acknowledging the body as a temple encourages a sense of reverence and respect for oneself. This perspective challenges cultural narratives that often focus on superficial beauty, encouraging instead a deeper, spiritual understanding of the body's purpose.

Overcoming Neglect and Self-Neglect

Depression and other mental health struggles can lead to neglect of physical well-being. Understanding the body as a temple can counteract these tendencies, providing a reason to care for oneself as a form of spiritual obedience. In times of difficulty, remembering that we are loved and valued by God can empower us to practice self-care, even when it feels challenging.

Relying on God's Strength

For many, maintaining physical health may feel overwhelming or difficult. The Bible reassures us that God provides strength in our weakness. Isaiah 40:29-31 says:

> "He gives strength to the weary and increases the power of the weak. Even youths grow tired and weary, and young men stumble and fall; but those who hope in the Lord

will renew their strength. They will soar on wings like eagles; they will run and not grow weary, they will walk and not be faint." (Isaiah 40:29-31, NIV)

This passage reminds us that we are not alone in our efforts. Through God's strength, we can find the resilience to care for ourselves, recognizing that doing so honors both Him and His creation.

A Sacred Responsibility

In sum, viewing the body as a temple reinforces the sacred responsibility we hold to care for ourselves holistically. Physical well-being is not a separate endeavor but part of a life devoted to God. As we nurture our bodies, we also nurture our spiritual lives, making ourselves better able to serve, love, and glorify God.

This perspective transforms physical self-care from an optional practice into an essential part of a faithful, God-centered life. By caring for our physical selves, we honor God, embrace His gifts, and prepare ourselves to live out the calling He has placed on our lives.

CHAPTER 03

SLEEP AS A PILLAR OF MENTAL HEALTH

Sleep is foundational to overall well-being, particularly mental health. Poor sleep disrupts the body's natural rhythms, leading to both physical and emotional consequences. For those dealing with depression, sleep can be both a challenge and a solution—either intensifying symptoms when inadequate or alleviating them when optimized. This chapter explores the critical role sleep plays in mental resilience and stability, examining the scientific, psychological, and biblical perspectives on the importance of rest.

The Science of Sleep and Depression

Sleep is a complex process essential for physical, emotional, and cognitive health. Research shows that sleep and mood are deeply connected; poor sleep not only affects physical health but also has significant psychological effects. When sleep is disrupted, the brain's ability to regulate mood, process information, and maintain energy levels is impaired.

1. Sleep and Mood Regulation: Sleep affects the brain's neurotransmitter levels, such as serotonin, dopamine, and norepinephrine, which influence mood, focus, and motivation. A deficiency in these neurotransmitters can lead to mood disorders, including depression.

2. Sleep and Cognitive Function: During sleep, the brain processes and consolidates memories, and a lack of quality sleep can lead to fogginess, decreased concentration, and impaired judgment. These effects can compound feelings of hopelessness or despair in individuals experiencing depression.

3. The Stress-Sleep Cycle: Poor sleep increases the release of stress hormones, like cortisol, which, in high levels, contribute to anxiety and exacerbate depressive symptoms. Conversely, sufficient sleep supports the body's natural ability to reduce stress.

In essence, sleep deprivation and depression often form a vicious cycle, where poor sleep worsens depression, and depressive symptoms make it harder to sleep. Understanding and prioritizing sleep as a key component of mental health management can provide both preventive and therapeutic benefits.

Biblical Insights on Rest and Renewal

The Bible speaks extensively about the importance of rest. From Genesis to the New Testament, rest is presented not only as necessary but as holy. God, in His creation of the world, sets an example by resting on the seventh day:

> "By the seventh day God had finished the work he had been doing; so on the seventh day he rested from all his work. Then God blessed the seventh day and made it holy, because on it he rested from all the work of creating that he had done." (Genesis 2:2-3, NIV)

God's example of rest underscores the importance of balance and renewal in life. Rest is more than just physical downtime; it's a way to honor the rhythms that God designed for human flourishing.

The Concept of Sabbath

The commandment to observe the Sabbath illustrates the significance of rest in the believer's life. In Exodus, God instructs His people:

> "Six days you shall labor, and do all your work, but the seventh day is a Sabbath to the Lord your God. On it you shall not do any work…" (Exodus 20:9-10, NIV)

The Sabbath is a time set aside for restoration, not only spiritually but physically and mentally. Taking this time for rest aligns with God's intent for us to rejuvenate, enabling us to serve Him and others with full strength. The Sabbath model reveals that regular, intentional rest is necessary and should not be neglected.

Practical Ways to Improve Sleep for Mental Health

Understanding the importance of sleep is the first step, but developing practical habits to achieve quality sleep is equally essential. Let's explore some evidence-based strategies that can improve sleep quality, particularly for individuals experiencing depression.

1. Set a Consistent Sleep Schedule: Going to bed and waking up at the same time each day helps regulate the body's internal clock. This consistency promotes better sleep quality and reduces the likelihood of insomnia or disturbed sleep.

Biblical Insight: Just as God establishes regular patterns in creation, from day and night to the Sabbath, maintaining a routine is part of aligning our lives with God's order. Ecclesiastes 3:1 reminds us, "There is a time for everything, and a season for every activity under the heavens" (Ecclesiastes 3:1, NIV).

2. Create a Calming Bedtime Routine: Incorporating relaxing activities before bed, such as reading, praying, or meditating, can prepare the mind and body for rest. Avoiding electronic devices at least an hour before bed can also reduce exposure to blue light, which interferes with sleep-inducing hormones like melatonin.

Biblical Insight: In Psalm 4:8, David expresses his confidence in the Lord's protection, allowing him to rest peacefully: "In peace I will lie down and sleep, for you alone,

Lord, make me dwell in safety" (Psalm 4:8, NIV). Approaching sleep with a spirit of peace and trust in God's protection can ease anxiety and prepare us for restful sleep.

3. Limit Stimulants and Avoid Alcohol Before Bed: Caffeine and alcohol can interfere with sleep quality. While caffeine disrupts sleep by blocking the sleep-promoting neurotransmitter adenosine, alcohol may initially cause drowsiness but disrupts deeper stages of sleep later in the night.

4. Exercise Regularly: Physical activity promotes better sleep, but it's advisable to avoid vigorous exercise close to bedtime. Morning or afternoon exercise supports the body's circadian rhythms, which can improve sleep quality at night.

5. Trust in God's Provision and Release Worries: For those dealing with depression, worry and anxiety can be barriers to restful sleep. The Bible encourages believers to cast their cares on God, trusting Him to provide peace. In 1 Peter 5:7, we read:

> "Cast all your anxiety on him because he cares for you." (1 Peter 5:7, NIV)

Practicing this spiritual discipline of releasing worries to God can be transformative, helping to calm the mind before bed.

Sleep as Spiritual Rejuvenation

In the Gospels, we see that Jesus valued rest, often retreating to quiet places to restore His strength through prayer and solitude. One notable instance is in Mark 6:31, where Jesus advises His disciples to rest:

> "Then, because so many people were coming and going that they did not even have a chance to eat, he said to them, 'Come with me by yourselves to a quiet place and get some rest.'" (Mark 6:31, NIV)

Jesus' example underscores the importance of periodic rest. Just as He took time to recharge, we too are encouraged to renew our strength. Viewing sleep as a form of spiritual rejuvenation can transform it from a mundane necessity into a divine practice.

The Role of Faith in Managing Sleeplessness

In times of stress and depression, sleeplessness can feel insurmountable. For believers, leaning on faith can be a source of comfort. The Psalmist reflects on this in Psalm 127:2:

> "In vain you rise early and stay up late, toiling for food to eat—for he grants sleep to those he loves." (Psalm 127:2, NIV)

This verse serves as a reminder that God desires rest for His people. Trusting in His provision allows us to release the burdens that prevent restful sleep, knowing that He is watching over us.

Addressing Sleep Disturbances from a Spiritual Perspective

Sometimes, despite best efforts, sleep remains elusive. Whether due to anxiety, stress, or the effects of depression, sleeplessness can be an overwhelming experience. In these moments, turning to prayer and meditation on Scripture can help create a peaceful mindset. Philippians 4:6-7 advises believers:

> "Do not be anxious about anything, but in every situation, by prayer and petition, with thanksgiving, present your requests to God. And the peace of God, which transcends all understanding, will guard your hearts and your minds in Christ Jesus." (Philippians 4:6-7, NIV)

Approaching sleep with prayerful trust in God's peace can shift the focus away from anxiety, allowing the mind to rest in His care.

Embracing Sleep as Part of God's Design

Finally, it's essential to view sleep as an intentional part of God's design for human life. Rather than viewing rest as merely a physical necessity, Scripture encourages us to embrace sleep as a God-given gift, integral to our mental and spiritual health.

The value of sleep aligns with the biblical call to care for the body as a temple. By prioritizing sleep, we not only benefit our mental well-being but also honor God's provision, enabling us to live fully and serve Him effectively. This perspective transforms the pursuit of quality sleep from a simple health recommendation into a holistic, faith-driven practice.

Sleep, as a pillar of mental health, is a precious gift from God, meant to restore, refresh, and equip us for His work. Whether viewed through the lens of science or Scripture, the importance of sleep cannot be overstated. By aligning our sleep habits with God's design, we enhance not only our mental resilience but also our spiritual connection with Him. Through rest, we find renewal, drawing closer to the peace and strength He freely offers.

Tips for Better Sleep

Good quality sleep is essential for both physical and mental health. For those experiencing depression, sleep becomes even more crucial, as poor sleep quality can exacerbate depressive symptoms. Creating a structured approach to sleep through consistency and relaxation helps restore the mind and body, promoting emotional resilience and mental well-being. In this chapter, we'll examine the psychological benefits of a consistent sleep schedule and a calming bedtime routine, along with practical tips to achieve both.

The Importance of a Consistent Sleep Schedule

Establishing a regular sleep schedule—going to bed and waking up at the same time every day—promotes a stable circadian rhythm, the body's natural 24-hour clock that regulates sleep-wake cycles. This internal clock influences hormone release, body temperature, and other bodily functions that are critical for sleep and mental health. A disrupted circadian rhythm can lead to irregular sleep patterns, causing mental fatigue and emotional instability, which are especially detrimental for individuals managing depression.

Psychological Impact of a Consistent Sleep Schedule

1. Improved Mood and Emotional Stability: When sleep becomes irregular, the brain's ability to regulate emotions is compromised. Consistent sleep schedules help maintain neurotransmitter levels—like serotonin and dopamine—that are essential for mood stabilization and stress management. Studies show that regular sleep helps to reduce the intensity of mood swings, alleviate irritability, and improve overall mood.

2. Reduced Risk of Insomnia: Irregular sleep schedules can lead to insomnia, as the brain becomes

uncertain about when to initiate the sleep process. A stable routine signals the brain to release melatonin, the hormone that promotes sleepiness, at the same time each evening, reducing the likelihood of lying awake at night.

3. Enhanced Cognitive Function: Cognitive functions such as memory, concentration, and problem-solving are all dependent on regular, restorative sleep. When the sleep schedule is consistent, the brain can effectively process and consolidate information, which is crucial for individuals experiencing depressive symptoms. Improved cognitive function also contributes to better decision-making and a reduced likelihood of negative thought patterns.

4. Lowered Stress and Anxiety: Maintaining a routine provides a sense of control and predictability, reducing feelings of stress and anxiety. For people dealing with depression, a structured sleep schedule can alleviate some of the chaos often associated with mental health struggles, making them feel more in control of their day-to-day lives.

Tips for Maintaining a Consistent Sleep Schedule

- Set a Fixed Bedtime and Wake-up Time: Even on weekends, try to stick to a regular schedule to strengthen your circadian rhythm.

- Limit Daytime Naps: If you need to nap, aim for a short nap (15-30 minutes) in the early afternoon. Long or late naps can interfere with nighttime sleep.

- Gradual Adjustments: If you need to reset your sleep schedule, make gradual adjustments by shifting your bedtime and wake-up time by 15-30 minutes each day until you reach your goal.

The Value of a Calming Bedtime Routine

A bedtime routine involves activities performed in the hour or so leading up to sleep, designed to signal to your body and mind that it's time to wind down. Creating a calming bedtime routine is especially beneficial for people with depression, as it can help them relax, minimize anxiety, and foster a more peaceful mindset before sleep.

Psychological Benefits of a Calming Bedtime Routine

1. Reduced Anxiety and Rumination: A calming bedtime routine encourages relaxation, reducing the likelihood of lying in bed with racing thoughts. For individuals with depression, bedtime can be a challenging period when negative thoughts intensify. By establishing a calming pre-sleep ritual, it becomes easier to focus on relaxing activities instead of ruminating on worries.

2. Enhanced Association Between Bedtime and Sleep: Over time, performing the same relaxing activities before bed strengthens the association between bedtime and sleep. This conditioning effect encourages the brain to recognize these

cues as signals to wind down, making it easier to fall asleep quickly.

3. Activation of the Parasympathetic Nervous System: The parasympathetic nervous system is responsible for "rest and digest" functions that counteract the body's stress response. Gentle, calming activities before bed, like reading or practicing deep breathing, activate this system, lowering heart rate and blood pressure and helping the body enter a relaxed state conducive to sleep.

4. Increased Feelings of Safety and Comfort: Depression can heighten feelings of insecurity or discomfort. A structured bedtime routine with comforting activities can create a sense of safety and peace, making it easier to release the day's stress and approach sleep with a calm mind.

Creating a Calming Bedtime Routine

Below are some evidence-based practices for developing a calming bedtime routine that promotes restful sleep and improves mental health.

- Dim the Lights: About an hour before bed, lower the lights to signal to your brain that it's time to start producing melatonin. Bright lights, especially blue light from electronic devices, can interfere with this process, making it harder to feel sleepy.

- Limit Screen Time: Electronic devices emit blue light, which suppresses melatonin and makes falling asleep more difficult. Aim to avoid screens for at least 30-60 minutes before bed. If screen use is unavoidable, consider using a blue light filter or wearing blue light-blocking glasses.

- Practice Relaxation Techniques: Engage in activities like deep breathing exercises, progressive muscle relaxation, or gentle yoga. These activities help activate the parasympathetic nervous system, lowering stress and preparing the mind for sleep.

- Journal or Reflect on Positive Moments: Journaling can serve as a mental release, helping to empty the mind of any lingering thoughts or anxieties. Additionally, reflecting on positive moments from the day can shift the focus away from worries, promoting a more positive mindset as you transition into sleep.

- Engage in Quiet Reading or Meditation: Reading a book (preferably not too stimulating) or practicing meditation can help calm the mind and establish a mental break from the day's activities. Meditation, especially, has been shown to reduce stress, improve emotional resilience, and increase self-awareness.

- Incorporate Prayer or Mindful Gratitude: For individuals who find comfort in faith or spirituality, bedtime can be an opportunity to engage in prayer or practice gratitude. Studies suggest that gratitude can improve sleep by reducing stress, fostering positive thoughts, and creating a sense of peace before bed.

The Role of Consistency and Relaxation in Managing Depression

Developing and maintaining a consistent sleep schedule and bedtime routine provides a foundation for mental and physical health. For those struggling with depression, these strategies not only improve sleep quality but also contribute to overall emotional resilience and stability. When practiced over time, these habits can help break the cycle of poor sleep and depressive symptoms, allowing individuals to face each day with renewed strength and focus.

A stable sleep pattern, combined with calming bedtime activities, can empower individuals to take an active role in managing their mental health. By prioritizing these practices, individuals can reclaim control over their sleep, cultivate emotional balance, and support their journey toward healing.

The Role of Rest in Religious Traditions

Rest holds a significant place across many religious traditions, seen not merely as a time of physical recuperation but as an essential spiritual practice. The notion of rest is woven through sacred texts and teachings, where it is portrayed as a divine commandment, a path to inner peace, and an avenue for reconnecting with the divine. In Christianity, the Sabbath is a day sanctified by God Himself, a day set apart for rest and worship. Other religious traditions also elevate rest as a period of restoration and contemplation, suggesting that rest serves to nourish not only the body but the soul and mind as well. In this chapter, we explore the theological implications of rest in religious texts, focusing on how this practice supports mental and spiritual well-being.

The Sabbath in the Judeo-Christian Tradition

The Sabbath, as a day of rest, is one of the most profound expressions of rest in religious literature. In the Bible, the Sabbath is introduced in Genesis as part of the creation narrative:

> "By the seventh day, God had finished the work he had been doing; so on the seventh day he rested from all his work. Then God blessed the seventh day and made it holy, because on it he rested from all the work of creating that he had done" (Genesis 2:2-3, NIV).

This passage signifies rest as an inherent part of creation. God, omnipotent and without fatigue, chose to rest, not out of necessity, but as an example for humankind. The act of rest sanctifies time, setting it apart as a moment to pause, reflect, and honor the Creator. Observing the Sabbath, therefore, becomes an invitation to imitate God by embracing rest and refraining from work, recognizing that life's rhythms include both labor and respite.

The commandment to observe the Sabbath is further emphasized in Exodus:

> "Remember the Sabbath day by keeping it holy. Six days you shall labor and do all your work, but the seventh day is a sabbath to the Lord your God. On it you shall not do any work" (Exodus 20:8-10, NIV).

In this passage, the Sabbath is presented as a gift from God, a day of rest intended to free individuals from the endless cycle of work. For the ancient Israelites, this commandment represented a radical departure from the labor-intensive lives they had endured in Egypt, offering them a taste of liberation and spiritual renewal.

Rest and the Restoration of the Soul

In the Psalms, rest is described as a means of restoring and renewing the soul. David, a central figure in the Old Testament, often expressed his dependence on rest to maintain his faith and sense of inner peace. One of the most well-known verses, Psalm 23, captures this sentiment:

> "The Lord is my shepherd; I shall not want. He makes me lie down in green pastures; he leads me beside still waters; he restores my soul" (Psalm 23:1-3, ESV).

Here, the act of resting in "green pastures" symbolizes peace and contentment, and God is portrayed as a shepherd who leads His followers toward places of spiritual renewal. This verse illustrates rest as an opportunity for God to heal the weary soul, providing a respite from life's anxieties. Rest is not just a physical necessity but also a divine act of restoration that replenishes the spirit.

The emphasis on spiritual renewal through rest can also be found in the teachings of Jesus. In the New Testament, He invites all who are weary to find rest in Him:

> "Come to me, all you who are weary and burdened, and I will give you rest" (Matthew 11:28, NIV).

This verse speaks to the broader theological view of rest as an act of surrender, a chance to hand over life's burdens to God. Jesus offers a rest that is not only physical but spiritual—a sanctuary for those overwhelmed by worry, exhaustion, and despair. This invitation to rest underscores the divine compassion of God, who understands human limitations and provides rest as a remedy for the soul.

Rest as a Commandment and a Gift

In Deuteronomy, the Sabbath commandment is restated with an added reminder of the Israelites' deliverance from slavery:

> "Observe the Sabbath day by keeping it holy, as the Lord your God has commanded you. Six days you shall labor and do all your work, but the seventh day is a sabbath to the Lord your God... Remember that you were slaves in Egypt and that the Lord your God brought you out of there with a mighty hand and an outstretched arm" (Deuteronomy 5:12-15, NIV).

Here, rest is presented as a reminder of freedom and divine deliverance. The Sabbath was a day to break free from the constraints of daily labor and to celebrate their liberation. This liberation theme implies that rest is more than mere relaxation; it is an acknowledgment of God's intervention and an opportunity to express gratitude. Rest, therefore, functions as both a command and a gift—a moment set apart to rejoice in God's love and mercy.

The Concept of Rest in Other Religious Traditions

While Christianity and Judaism emphasize the Sabbath, other religious traditions also regard rest as vital to spiritual life. In Islam, for instance, the concept of rest is implicit in the rhythm of daily prayers. Each of the five prayers punctuates the day with moments of pause and spiritual reflection, creating intervals for mental and emotional rest. Furthermore, the Holy Quran describes night as a time of rest, created for humans to rejuvenate:

> "And We made your sleep [a means for] rest. And We made the night as clothing" (Quran 78:9-10, Sahih International).

In this verse, sleep and nighttime are presented as intentional gifts from God, designed to provide physical and mental respite. The emphasis on rest suggests a divine understanding of human needs and limitations, highlighting rest as an essential part of life.

In Hinduism, rest is woven into the practice of meditation and mindfulness. The sacred texts encourage individuals to meditate and withdraw from worldly concerns, achieving inner peace and self-awareness. This inward focus allows practitioners to experience mental rest and spiritual clarity, reinforcing the belief that rest is not only physical but also a mental discipline that brings one closer to the divine.

How Rest Nourishes the Soul and Mind

The theological foundation for rest across these religious traditions points to its profound impact on mental and spiritual well-being. Rest is viewed as more than just a cessation of work; it is a deliberate act of stepping away from the demands of the world and focusing on the self and one's relationship with God.

1. Rest as an Act of Faith: Choosing to rest is a demonstration of faith, an acknowledgment that the world

does not rely on human efforts alone. By resting, individuals place their trust in God's provision and care, recognizing that their worth is not solely based on productivity.

2. Rest as Spiritual Rejuvenation: The act of rest provides space for introspection, gratitude, and reconnection with divine purpose. Whether through prayer, meditation, or Sabbath observance, rest nourishes the soul, allowing individuals to feel grounded and re-centered in their faith.

3. Rest as a Reminder of Divine Compassion: Religious texts depict rest as a compassionate provision from God, given for the benefit of human well-being. Observing rest, therefore, becomes an acknowledgment of God's kindness and care, reinforcing the belief that God understands human needs and has provided ways to meet them.

4. Rest as a Path to Inner Peace: Regular periods of rest promote emotional balance and inner peace. By taking time to rest, individuals can release their anxieties, finding solace in the knowledge that God's love is constant and sustaining. This peace becomes a source of strength that carries through even the most challenging times.

Embracing Rest as a Spiritual Discipline

Rest is a fundamental aspect of religious life that transcends physical relaxation, fostering mental resilience and spiritual growth. By observing rest in accordance with sacred teachings, individuals engage in a profound act of faith, one that reaffirms their dependence on God and restores their inner peace. In a world that often values productivity above all else, religious traditions call believers to a higher understanding of rest—a space where they can lay down their burdens, renew their spirits, and reconnect with the divine.

In embracing rest as a spiritual discipline, individuals are reminded that they are not defined by their accomplishments but by their inherent worth as creations of God. Observing rest with intention and gratitude, they align themselves with the rhythm of life established by God Himself, embodying a faith that values peace, rejuvenation, and divine connection. Through this understanding of rest, believers find solace and strength, knowing that in their moments of stillness, they are held by the divine embrace of their Creator.

Let us delve deeper into the concept of rest through an expository Bible study approach, utilizing Strong's Concordance to unpack key terms and phrases that illuminate rest's profound role in religious traditions. This study seeks to emphasize rest as both a spiritual commandment and a divine invitation, offering readers a deeper understanding of rest's transformative power for the mind, body, and soul.

The Biblical Foundation of Rest: A Study with Strong's Concordance

To understand the theological depth of rest, we must examine the Hebrew and Greek words for "rest" used throughout the Bible. Each word sheds light on various dimensions of rest, from physical cessation to spiritual renewal.

1. Hebrew Word "Shabbat" (שָׁבַת) - Strong's H7673

The term "Shabbat," translated as "Sabbath" in English, originates from the Hebrew root word "shabat," meaning "to cease" or "to rest." This root word, used in Genesis 2:2-3, is directly tied to the Sabbath commandment. God rested (shabat) on the seventh day after creating the heavens and the earth, setting a precedent for His people to pause from labor and dedicate time to reflection and worship. The Sabbath, therefore, is more than an instruction for physical rest; it is a designated time for honoring God's creative work and experiencing renewal.

Expository Insight:

In observing the Sabbath, believers reflect God's image by engaging in rest, showing that creation's rhythm includes both work and pause. This cessation from labor isn't merely physical but embodies a deeper spiritual reflection, enabling us to reset and renew our faith.

2. Hebrew Word "Nuach" (נוּחַ) - Strong's H5117

Another Hebrew word, "nuach," meaning "to settle down, rest, or be quiet," appears in Exodus 33:14, where God says, "My presence shall go with you, and I will give you rest" (Exodus 33:14, ESV). Here, "nuach" signifies a peace and rest that come directly from God's presence. Unlike physical rest alone, "nuach" encompasses a sense of divine calm, where the soul can find comfort in God's presence.

Expository Insight:

The concept of "nuach" is an invitation to experience a divine peace that surpasses understanding. This rest is not just an absence of labor; it is a transformative encounter with God, where His presence calms the heart and soul. Such rest fulfills a spiritual need, reminding believers of God's companionship and comfort in every life stage.

3. Greek Word "Anapauo" (ἀναπαύω) - Strong's G373

In the New Testament, the Greek term "anapauo" is often used to convey rest. In Matthew 11:28, Jesus extends His famous invitation: "Come to me, all who labor and are heavy laden, and I will give you rest." Here, "anapauo" means "to refresh or give rest." Jesus promises not only relief from burdens but a spiritual rejuvenation that only He can provide.

Expository Insight:

Jesus' invitation in Matthew 11:28 highlights the rest available to believers who turn to Him amid life's stresses.

This rest is a restoration of the soul—a spiritual renewal that lifts the weight of worries. Unlike physical rest, "anapauo" reflects a deeper, transformative peace that Christ offers, making Him the source of true rest and restoration.

The Sabbath Rest as a Covenant Sign

In the Old Testament, God's commandment to observe the Sabbath was given to Israel as a unique sign of their covenant relationship with Him:

> "It is a sign between me and the children of Israel forever: for in six days the Lord made heaven and earth, and on the seventh day he rested, and was refreshed" (Exodus 31:17, KJV).

The Sabbath is not just an individual practice but a communal one. Strong's Concordance explains "refreshed" in this context as "naphash" (Strong's H5314), which implies "to take breath" or "to revive." God's people collectively embrace the Sabbath as a way to breathe deeply in the presence of the Creator, experiencing a shared renewal that unites them with Him.

Expository Insight:

The Sabbath as a covenantal sign serves to distinguish Israel as God's people, a reminder of their liberation from slavery and a weekly renewal of their dependence on Him. Observing the Sabbath is not merely a ritual but a testament of faith, a reminder that God provides for His people as they release control, trusting in His provision and timing.

Jesus as the Fulfillment of the Sabbath

In the New Testament, Jesus shifts the focus from strict Sabbath observance to understanding Him as the ultimate source of rest:

> "For the Son of Man is Lord of the Sabbath" (Matthew 12:8, NIV).

Here, Jesus proclaims His authority over the Sabbath, redefining rest as something rooted in relationship with Him rather than in the observance of rituals. The Greek word "sabbatismos" (σαββατισμός) in Hebrews 4:9-10 refers to a "Sabbath rest" available to believers who trust in Jesus. This "sabbatismos" is not restricted to a day but represents a continual rest found in faith.

Expository Insight:

Hebrews 4:9-10 reveals the Sabbath's true essence as a symbol of salvation through Christ. This "rest" is a state of soul, a spiritual repose that believers experience by trusting in Jesus' finished work. Observing Sabbath principles transcends mere ritualistic practice, inviting believers to a lifestyle of peace in Him.

Rest as an Act of Faith and Obedience

Rest is a powerful act of obedience and faith, especially when life's demands push us toward constant busyness. Choosing to rest signifies our reliance on God rather than on ourselves:

> "Be still, and know that I am God" (Psalm 46:10, NIV).

The phrase "be still" is translated from the Hebrew "raphah" (Strong's H7503), meaning "to let go, to cease striving." By resting, we acknowledge that God is in control, releasing our burdens and placing our trust in His sovereignty. This act of stillness becomes an exercise in faith, a spiritual discipline that keeps believers grounded in God's providence.

Expository Insight:

The call to "be still" encourages a mindful cessation of self-reliance, guiding believers to seek strength and peace in God's presence. This rest promotes emotional and spiritual resilience, a reminder that even in life's storms, God's steadfastness remains. Rest, therefore, becomes both a statement of faith and a source of comfort.

Rest as an Essential Spiritual Discipline

From Genesis to the teachings of Jesus, rest is presented as a sacred practice woven into the fabric of creation. Observing rest, whether through Sabbath observance, quiet meditation, or mindful cessation, is a spiritual discipline that honors God's design for humanity. By turning to God for true rest, believers experience a peace that surpasses understanding, a rejuvenation that fuels their daily lives.

In practicing rest, we honor the body as a temple, nurture our spirits, and align ourselves with the divine rhythm established by God. This rest is not just a cessation of work; it is a surrender to God's love, a trust in His provision, and a source of lasting peace for the soul.

In conclusion, rest serves as both a command and a gift, a call to pause and acknowledge the Creator's presence in every moment of life. As we integrate rest into our routines, we find that it does more than restore us physically; it transforms us spiritually, providing the resilience and faith needed to face life's challenges with renewed hope and strength.

CHAPTER 04

THE POWER OF NUTRITION FOR EMOTIONAL HEALTH

The relationship between nutrition and emotional health has gained increasing attention in recent years. Just as food choices impact physical well-being, they also play a significant role in mental health. Researchers have found compelling evidence linking certain nutrients with improved mood, reduced stress, and greater emotional resilience. This chapter explores how specific foods and nutrients support brain health, the mechanisms through which they affect mood, and practical dietary recommendations for emotional wellness.

Understanding the Link Between Diet and Depression

Depression and other mood disorders are multifaceted conditions influenced by a combination of biological, psychological, and social factors. Nutrition, however, is one factor that directly influences the brain's functioning and can play a significant role in either exacerbating or alleviating depressive symptoms. Emerging research suggests that individuals with nutrient-poor diets—high in processed foods, sugars, and unhealthy fats—are more susceptible to mood disorders. Conversely, those who consume nutrient-dense foods rich in vitamins, minerals, and essential fatty acids tend to have better mental health outcomes.

The "gut-brain axis," which refers to the communication pathway between the gut and the brain, is also a key factor. A healthy gut microbiome can positively impact neurotransmitter production, particularly serotonin, which regulates mood. In fact, about 90% of serotonin, often called the "feel-good" hormone, is produced in the gut. Consequently, a nutritious diet can help foster a healthy gut, which, in turn, can support a balanced mood.

Nutrient-Rich Foods That Improve Mood and Support Brain Health

1. Omega-3 Fatty Acids

Omega-3 fatty acids are essential fats that play a significant role in brain health. Studies have shown that these fats, especially eicosapentaenoic acid (EPA) and docosahexaenoic acid (DHA), are crucial for maintaining healthy cell membranes in the brain and regulating neurotransmitters like dopamine and serotonin, both of which affect mood.

Sources: Fatty fish (salmon, sardines, mackerel), walnuts, chia seeds, and flaxseeds.

Evidence: A meta-analysis published in Translational Psychiatry concluded that omega-3 supplements can have a small to moderate effect in alleviating depressive symptoms, particularly in individuals with major depressive disorder. The anti-inflammatory properties of omega-3s are believed to contribute to their mood-enhancing effects.

2. Complex Carbohydrates

Carbohydrates are essential for brain function and mood regulation, as they help produce serotonin. However, it's crucial to choose complex carbohydrates, which provide a slow, steady release of glucose, rather than simple carbohydrates, which can lead to blood sugar spikes and subsequent mood crashes.

Sources: Whole grains (oats, brown rice, quinoa), legumes, fruits, and vegetables.

Evidence: Studies show that a low glycemic index diet (consisting of complex carbohydrates) stabilizes blood sugar levels, which can reduce mood swings and feelings of irritability. A stable blood sugar level also minimizes the stress response, contributing to a calmer mood.

3. B Vitamins

B vitamins, particularly B6, B9 (folate), and B12, are crucial for brain health and the production of neurotransmitters. Folate and B12, for example, are involved in synthesizing serotonin and dopamine, which influence mood and emotion.

Sources: Leafy greens, legumes, nuts, seeds, eggs, and fortified grains.

Evidence: A study published in Journal of Psychiatric Research found that individuals with low levels of B vitamins were more likely to experience depressive symptoms. Folate, in particular, has been associated with reduced depression severity, likely due to its role in serotonin production.

4. Antioxidant-Rich Foods

Antioxidants help combat oxidative stress and inflammation, both of which have been linked to depression. Vitamins C and E, as well as beta-carotene, neutralize free radicals that can damage brain cells over time.

Sources: Berries (blueberries, strawberries), citrus fruits, nuts, seeds, spinach, and broccoli.

Evidence: Studies suggest that diets rich in antioxidants may help alleviate depressive symptoms. For instance, research in Frontiers in Psychology highlighted that individuals with higher dietary antioxidant intake had a lower incidence of depressive symptoms.

5. Magnesium

Magnesium plays a role in more than 300 biochemical reactions in the body, including those that regulate mood. It helps manage the stress response and is often referred to as the "relaxation mineral" because of its calming effects.

Sources: Leafy greens, nuts, seeds, whole grains, and legumes.

Evidence: A review published in Nutrients found a correlation between low magnesium levels and depressive symptoms. Supplementing magnesium, particularly in individuals with magnesium deficiency, was associated with improved mood.

6. Probiotics and Fermented Foods

A healthy gut microbiome supports emotional well-being through the gut-brain axis. Probiotics, or beneficial bacteria, promote gut health, which is essential for neurotransmitter production and a balanced mood.

Sources: Yogurt, kefir, sauerkraut, kimchi, and kombucha.

Evidence: A randomized controlled trial published in Psychiatry Research showed that individuals who consumed probiotics reported lower stress and anxiety levels.

This suggests that improving gut health through probiotic-rich foods can have a positive impact on mood and emotional health.

7. Tryptophan-Rich Foods

Tryptophan is an amino acid that serves as a precursor to serotonin, a neurotransmitter linked to mood regulation. Consuming tryptophan-rich foods can help support serotonin production in the brain.

Sources: Turkey, chicken, dairy products, nuts, seeds, and tofu.

Evidence: Research suggests that diets with adequate tryptophan can improve mood and reduce irritability. A study in Nutritional Neuroscience found that individuals with higher tryptophan intake reported lower symptoms of depression and anxiety.

Practical Dietary Recommendations for Emotional Health

1. Focus on Whole, Unprocessed Foods

Diets high in processed foods, sugars, and unhealthy fats have been linked to higher rates of depression and anxiety. Instead, focus on whole foods that provide essential nutrients without added preservatives or sugars.

2. Incorporate a Variety of Nutrient-Dense Foods

A diverse diet ensures that you receive a wide range of vitamins, minerals, and other nutrients that support brain health. Variety also makes it easier to sustain dietary changes over the long term.

3. Maintain Balanced Blood Sugar Levels

Eating smaller, regular meals that include complex carbohydrates, healthy fats, and protein can help stabilize blood sugar levels. This reduces mood swings and maintains consistent energy throughout the day.

4. Stay Hydrated

Dehydration can lead to irritability and fatigue, both of which can exacerbate depressive symptoms. Aim for adequate water intake daily to support overall brain function.

5. Limit Sugar and Processed Foods

Processed foods and high sugar intake can lead to inflammation, which has been linked to depression. Instead, opt for natural sugars from fruits and avoid sugary snacks or drinks.

Understanding the link between diet and emotional health empowers individuals to make informed choices about what they eat, recognizing that food plays a crucial role in supporting mental well-being. By prioritizing nutrient-dense foods, individuals can positively influence their mood, reduce stress, and support brain health. Integrating these dietary principles as part of a holistic approach to managing depression can provide both physical and emotional benefits, supporting overall mental resilience.

Foods to Include and Avoid for Mental Health

Food choices have a profound effect on overall health, influencing not only physical well-being but also mental health. Studies increasingly highlight the critical role diet plays in managing mood, energy, and even symptoms of mental health disorders like depression and anxiety. In this chapter, we will explore which foods to include in a diet for emotional wellness, which foods to avoid, and sample meal ideas for incorporating these beneficial choices into daily life.

The Foundation: Emphasizing Whole Foods

Whole foods—those that are minimally processed, free of additives, and close to their natural form—are at the heart of a mentally healthy diet. Unlike processed foods, whole foods provide essential vitamins, minerals, and other nutrients without preservatives or excess sugars and unhealthy fats that can disrupt mood stability.

Key Benefits of Whole Foods for Mental Health:

- Nutrient Density: Whole foods are packed with vitamins, minerals, antioxidants, and fiber that support brain function and mood regulation.

- Reduced Inflammation: Processed foods can lead to inflammation, which has been linked to depression. Whole foods, in contrast, reduce inflammation and support overall health.

- Stable Blood Sugar Levels: Whole foods, especially when combined with fiber, protein, and healthy fats, promote steady blood sugar, preventing energy crashes that often lead to irritability or low mood.

Foods to Include

1. Fruits and Vegetables

Fruits and vegetables are essential for a healthy mind and body, providing a rich source of antioxidants, fiber, vitamins, and minerals.

- Berries: Blueberries, strawberries, and raspberries are loaded with antioxidants that combat oxidative stress in the brain, which is linked to depression.

- Leafy Greens: Spinach, kale, and Swiss chard are high in folate, a B vitamin crucial for brain health.

- Citrus Fruits: Oranges and lemons are rich in vitamin C, which is essential for mood regulation and immune support.

Sample Diet Ideas: Start your day with a smoothie made from mixed berries, spinach, and a dash of Greek yogurt. Snack on carrot sticks or apple slices with almond butter.

2. Whole Grains

Whole grains, like brown rice, oats, and quinoa, are complex carbohydrates that provide a steady release of energy and help produce serotonin, the neurotransmitter associated with mood stabilization.

- Oats: Rich in fiber, they provide a steady release of energy and are known to reduce cholesterol and improve gut health.

- Quinoa: A complete protein, quinoa provides all essential amino acids, which are important for neurotransmitter production.

Sample Diet Ideas: Enjoy a bowl of oatmeal topped with fruit and a sprinkle of nuts in the morning, or try a quinoa and vegetable salad for lunch.

3. Healthy Fats

Healthy fats, particularly omega-3 fatty acids, are essential for brain health. They play a critical role in supporting the structure of brain cells and influencing mood-regulating neurotransmitters.

- Fatty Fish: Salmon, sardines, and mackerel are high in EPA and DHA, which help reduce inflammation and support mood.

- Avocados: Contain healthy monounsaturated fats, B vitamins, and potassium, which support nerve function and reduce stress.

Sample Diet Ideas: Have a salmon fillet with roasted vegetables for dinner, or add avocado slices to a whole-grain toast or salad.

4. Lean Proteins

Proteins, made of amino acids, are necessary for neurotransmitter synthesis, which is vital for mood regulation.

- Chicken and Turkey: High in tryptophan, which helps produce serotonin, leading to improved mood.

- Legumes: Beans and lentils are rich in protein, fiber, and complex carbohydrates, which help stabilize blood sugar.

Sample Diet Ideas: Prepare a lentil stew with mixed vegetables, or enjoy a grilled chicken salad with a variety of fresh vegetables.

5. Nuts and Seeds

Nuts and seeds provide healthy fats, fiber, and magnesium, which are all crucial for brain health.

- Walnuts: Known to be particularly beneficial due to their omega-3 content.

- Pumpkin Seeds: High in magnesium, which can help reduce symptoms of anxiety and depression.

Sample Diet Ideas: Snack on a handful of mixed nuts and seeds throughout the day, or sprinkle pumpkin seeds on top of salads or oatmeal.

6. Fermented Foods

Fermented foods promote gut health, which is directly connected to mood and mental health through the gut-brain axis.

- Yogurt with Live Cultures: Contains probiotics that improve gut health and, by extension, mood.

- Kimchi and Sauerkraut: These fermented vegetables are rich in probiotics and can improve gut flora diversity.

Sample Diet Ideas: Add a serving of yogurt with live cultures as a snack, or include a small portion of sauerkraut as a side dish.

Foods to Avoid

1. Processed Sugars

Sugar, especially in refined and added forms, can cause blood sugar spikes and crashes, leading to irritability, mood swings, and fatigue. Diets high in sugar can also lead to inflammation, which is associated with depression.

- Examples: Sodas, candies, pastries, and other processed sweets.

- Alternative: Use natural sweeteners like honey or maple syrup in moderation, or enjoy fruits for a sweet, nutrient-rich snack.

2. Refined Carbohydrates

Like sugars, refined carbs cause rapid blood sugar fluctuations, which can negatively impact mood.

- Examples: White bread, pasta, and baked goods made with white flour.

- Alternative: Replace with whole-grain options like whole wheat bread, brown rice, and whole-grain pasta.

3. Trans Fats and Highly Processed Fats

Trans fats, often found in fried and heavily processed foods, can increase inflammation and interfere with brain health.

- Examples: Fast food, margarine, and snacks made with hydrogenated oils.

- Alternative: Use olive oil or coconut oil for cooking, and opt for foods that are baked or grilled instead of fried.

4. Alcohol

Alcohol is a depressant that can disrupt sleep and worsen symptoms of depression and anxiety. It interferes with neurotransmitter balance and increases dehydration, which can worsen mood disorders.

- Alternative: Try herbal teas, flavored water, or mocktails as refreshing alternatives.

5. Caffeine (In Excess)

While moderate caffeine can enhance alertness, excessive caffeine can lead to anxiety, irritability, and sleep disruptions, which can exacerbate symptoms of depression.

- Examples: Energy drinks, excessive coffee consumption.

- Alternative: Try green tea or herbal teas for a gentler boost, or reduce coffee intake to moderate levels.

Sample Daily Diet Plan for Emotional Wellness

Breakfast:

- Oatmeal topped with blueberries, a handful of walnuts, and a drizzle of honey.

- Herbal tea or a small cup of coffee.

Mid-Morning Snack:

- Greek yogurt with a sprinkle of chia seeds and a few slices of banana.

Lunch:

- Quinoa salad with mixed vegetables (spinach, bell peppers, cucumbers), grilled chicken, and a handful of pumpkin seeds.

- Olive oil and lemon dressing.

Afternoon Snack:

- Apple slices with almond butter or a handful of mixed nuts and seeds.

Dinner:

- Baked salmon fillet with a side of steamed broccoli, sweet potato, and a small portion of sauerkraut.

- Glass of water or herbal tea.

Evening Snack (Optional):

- A small bowl of mixed berries or a slice of dark chocolate (70% or higher).

A balanced diet that emphasizes whole foods, lean proteins, complex carbohydrates, healthy fats, and probiotics can have a profound impact on emotional well-being. While food alone is not a cure for depression, nutrition serves as a powerful, complementary tool in the management of mood disorders. By reducing intake of processed sugars, refined carbohydrates, trans fats, and alcohol, individuals can avoid many triggers that can worsen mental health. Developing a nutrient-rich, balanced approach to eating is a practical and proactive step toward improving emotional health and overall well-being.

Eating Mindfully

In our busy lives, eating has often become a rushed, automatic act. However, practicing mindfulness while eating—paying close attention to each bite and savoring the sensory experience—can significantly improve both physical and mental well-being. Mindful eating helps individuals develop a healthier relationship with food, reduce stress, and even enhance the nutritional impact of their meals, which collectively contributes to improved mental health and emotional resilience.

The Psychological Perspective on Mindful Eating

Mindful eating draws on principles from mindfulness psychology, which encourages awareness of the present moment. Originating in Eastern practices like Buddhism, mindfulness has now been widely recognized in psychological science for its ability to improve mental health, manage stress, and promote emotional stability. Research shows that mindful eating can help reduce stress-related overeating, improve digestion, and foster positive eating behaviors. Moreover, this practice can counteract negative eating patterns, such as emotional eating, that are often linked to mental health issues like depression and anxiety.

When we engage in mindful eating, we give ourselves the opportunity to slow down, appreciate the meal before us, and connect with our internal signals of hunger and fullness. Here's a breakdown of the psychological benefits of mindful eating and how to incorporate it into daily life.

Psychological Benefits of Mindful Eating

1. Enhanced Awareness of Eating Patterns

Mindful eating helps us tune into the reasons behind our eating habits. Are we eating because we're truly hungry, or is it due to stress, boredom, or emotional discomfort? Often, emotional eating is an attempt to numb or distract from difficult emotions. By cultivating awareness, we can better distinguish between true hunger and emotional cravings, making it easier to manage our diet healthily.

Studies have found that mindful eating can significantly reduce emotional eating by helping individuals recognize triggers and make conscious choices, rather than reacting impulsively to emotions or stressors. Over time, this practice promotes a greater sense of control and agency over food choices.

2. Reduced Anxiety and Depression Symptoms

Mindfulness has been extensively studied for its positive effects on mental health, particularly for reducing symptoms of anxiety and depression. Eating mindfully has a similar benefit, as it encourages slowing down and engaging fully with the present moment. This practice interrupts the cycle of automatic, negative thinking that often accompanies anxiety and depression, making it a grounding experience.

When individuals eat mindfully, they can focus on the sensory experiences of eating—texture, taste, aroma, and appearance—allowing them to feel more connected to their food. This can have a calming effect, helping reduce feelings of stress or overwhelm. Moreover, practicing mindfulness has been linked to increased levels of serotonin, a neurotransmitter that plays a key role in mood regulation.

3. Better Digestion and Nutrient Absorption

The mind and body are intricately connected, and our mental state affects our physical processes, including digestion. Eating under stress or in a hurry can disrupt digestion, leading to discomfort and decreased nutrient absorption. When we eat mindfully, our body enters a relaxed state that supports healthy digestion and allows for the efficient absorption of nutrients. This not only enhances physical health but also provides the body and brain with the essential nutrients needed to support mental well-being.

4. Improved Self-Compassion and Relationship with Food

Mindful eating also encourages self-compassion, as it encourages an attitude of non-judgment. Instead of labeling foods as "good" or "bad," we approach eating with curiosity, acceptance, and kindness. Self-compassion is crucial in mental health, as it reduces self-criticism and helps individuals develop a balanced relationship with food.

Over time, mindful eating can reduce feelings of guilt or shame around food, which are common in individuals who struggle with emotional eating. Instead, individuals learn to enjoy food and listen to their body's needs without judgment. This positive relationship with food fosters an overall sense of well-being and mental stability.

Practicing Mindful Eating: Practical Steps

Here are some key practices that can help cultivate mindfulness while eating:

1. Take a Few Deep Breaths Before Eating

Before you begin eating, pause for a moment to take a few deep breaths. This simple act can help calm the mind, transition from a busy state to a relaxed one, and bring your attention to the present moment. Deep breathing signals to the body that it is time to relax, which aids in digestion and prepares you to focus on your meal.

2. Express Gratitude for Your Food

Taking a moment to appreciate the food before you can enhance the experience of eating mindfully. Reflecting on where the food came from, who prepared it, and how it will nourish your body fosters a sense of gratitude. Gratitude is also associated with greater life satisfaction and reduced stress, contributing to an overall improvement in mental well-being.

3. Engage All Five Senses

Mindful eating involves noticing the appearance, smell, taste, texture, and even the sound of food. Observing food with all five senses can deepen your connection to the experience. For instance, appreciate the vibrant colors on your plate, inhale the aroma, feel the texture with your fork, and listen to the sounds as you chew. This practice slows down the eating process and heightens your awareness of the meal.

4. Take Small Bites and Chew Thoroughly

Eating slowly and chewing thoroughly are essential components of mindful eating. By taking small bites and chewing each one at least 20 times, you give your body the chance to recognize feelings of fullness and prevent overeating. Eating slowly also allows the digestive process to work optimally and provides time to savor each bite.

5. Put Down Your Utensils Between Bites

Resting your utensils between bites is another effective way to pace yourself and avoid eating on "autopilot." Putting down your fork or spoon allows you to pause and appreciate each bite before reaching for the next one. This habit fosters awareness and gives you the time to consider whether you're still hungry or if you're satisfied.

6. Check In with Your Hunger and Fullness Cues

Throughout the meal, periodically check in with your hunger and fullness levels. Mindful eating encourages tuning into your body's signals instead of external cues (like finishing what's on the plate). By listening to your body's natural signals, you learn to eat until you feel satisfied, not overly full, which supports a balanced relationship with food.

7. Notice Emotional Responses Without Judgment

While eating, you may notice certain emotions arise, whether it's stress, contentment, or something else. Instead of reacting to these emotions by eating faster or reaching for comfort food, simply acknowledge these feelings without judgment. Observing emotional responses in this way can help you build resilience, prevent emotional eating, and foster a healthier mental state.

Sample Mindful Eating Exercise

Here's a step-by-step mindful eating exercise you can try with any snack or meal:

1. Choose a small portion of food, such as a handful of almonds or a piece of fruit.

2. Take a deep breath, calming yourself before beginning.

3. Observe the food visually—its color, shape, and texture.

4. Inhale deeply, noticing the smell of the food.

5. Take a small bite, chewing slowly and savoring the flavors and textures.

6. Pause between bites to check in with your hunger and fullness levels.

7. Continue eating slowly and mindfully until you feel satisfied, not overly full.

Mindful eating is a valuable practice for anyone seeking to improve their mental health and develop a healthier relationship with food. By slowing down and engaging all senses, mindful eating reduces stress, enhances nutrient absorption, and fosters a sense of satisfaction and gratitude. This approach not only benefits physical health but also supports emotional resilience and mental clarity. Incorporating mindful eating into daily routines can lead to a more balanced, fulfilling, and healthy relationship with food, nurturing both body and mind.

Spirituality and Nourishment

Food holds a profound place in spiritual traditions, often symbolizing blessings, sustenance, and connection to the divine. The act of nourishing our bodies is not only physical but can also be deeply spiritual. Through food, we experience God's provision, and by eating with gratitude, we honor the Creator who sustains us. This chapter will explore the spiritual significance of nourishment and how feeding the body can be an act of thanksgiving and reverence for God's ongoing care.

The Spiritual Meaning of Food in Scripture

Food is frequently mentioned in the Bible, symbolizing God's provision, blessing, and care for His people. In both the Old and New Testaments, food represents more than physical sustenance; it is also a sign of God's covenant, abundance, and loving kindness.

1. Food as Divine Provision

In the Old Testament, God's provision of manna in the wilderness is a powerful example of nourishment as a gift from God. As the Israelites journeyed through the desert, God provided them with "bread from heaven" to sustain them.

> "Then the Lord said to Moses, 'Behold, I will rain bread from heaven for you, and the people shall go out and gather a day's portion every day, that I may test them, whether they will walk in my law or not.'" – Exodus 16:4 (ESV)

God's gift of manna teaches us that every meal we receive is a blessing. As we consume food, we are reminded of His care and provision, both physically and spiritually. Nourishing our bodies with food can be an act of faith, trusting in God's continuous care.

2. Food as a Blessing and Celebration

Throughout the Bible, food often accompanies celebrations, signifying abundance and joy. For example, feasts were central to Israelite life and were commanded by God as part of worship and remembrance. The Passover meal, a sacred celebration, not only sustained the Israelites physically but reminded them of God's deliverance from Egypt.

> "And you shall observe this event as an ordinance for you and your children forever. When you enter the land which the Lord will give you, as He has promised, you shall observe this rite." – Exodus 12:24-25 (NASB)

Feasts like Passover underscore the importance of food as a way to honor God and remember His faithfulness. In a similar way, when we approach meals with a heart of gratitude, our everyday nourishment can become an act of worship, a celebration of the goodness God provides.

3. Jesus as the Bread of Life

In the New Testament, Jesus Himself uses food as a metaphor to convey spiritual truths. In John 6, He declares, "I am the bread of life," connecting the physical nourishment of bread with the eternal sustenance He offers.

> "Jesus said to them, 'I am the bread of life; whoever comes to me shall not hunger, and whoever believes in me shall never thirst.'" – John 6:35 (ESV)

Jesus emphasizes that while physical food sustains our bodies temporarily, only He can fulfill our spiritual hunger. Eating mindfully, with gratitude and reverence, can serve as a reminder of our dependence on Christ, the true source of life.

Nourishment as an Act of Gratitude

In a world that often takes food for granted, recognizing its source and giving thanks is a powerful act of humility and worship. Acknowledging that God is the ultimate provider elevates our eating to an act of gratitude and trust.

1. Prayers of Thanksgiving

In the Bible, meals are often preceded by blessings and prayers. Jesus consistently gave thanks before breaking bread, showing us that gratitude is an essential part of receiving nourishment.

> "And he took bread, gave thanks and broke it, and gave it to them, saying, 'This is my body given for you; do this in remembrance of me.'" – Luke 22:19 (NIV)

By pausing to give thanks, we center ourselves on God and acknowledge His hand in our lives. This act of gratitude transforms our relationship with food, reminding us that every meal is a gift from Him.

2. Mindful Eating as an Act of Worship

Eating mindfully is a way to appreciate the flavors, textures, and aromas of food, recognizing the intricate design of God's creation. When we eat slowly and savor each bite, we honor the Creator who has crafted these blessings.

Psalm 34:8 encourages us to "taste and see that the Lord is good," connecting our sensory experience with a deeper spiritual understanding. In taking time to appreciate what God provides, we are drawn into His presence and reminded of His kindness.

> "The earth is the Lord's, and everything in it, the world, and all who live in it." – Psalm 24:1 (NIV)

Recognizing that all of creation belongs to God deepens our gratitude and makes every meal an opportunity to celebrate His goodness.

The Theology of the Body as a Temple

Our bodies are described in the New Testament as temples of the Holy Spirit, deserving of care and respect. Nourishing the body, therefore, is not only an act of gratitude but also an act of honoring God with our physical health.

1. Honoring the Temple of the Holy Spirit

> "Do you not know that your body is a temple of the Holy Spirit within you, whom you have from God? You are not your own, for you were bought with a price. So glorify God in your body." – 1 Corinthians 6:19-20 (ESV)

This passage highlights that our bodies are not merely our own but are indwelt by the Holy Spirit. Taking care of ourselves through nutritious food and mindful eating is a way to glorify God, treating our bodies with the respect they deserve as His dwelling place.

2. Healthy Eating as Stewardship

Just as we are called to be stewards of the earth, we are also called to be good stewards of our bodies. The Bible encourages moderation, self-control, and respect for the body. By choosing nourishing foods, we demonstrate responsibility and self-control, honoring God's creation.

> "Whether you eat or drink, or whatever you do, do all to the glory of God." – 1 Corinthians 10:31 (ESV)

This verse serves as a reminder that even our most mundane actions can be expressions of faith. Eating healthily becomes an act of stewardship, an intentional choice to care for the body God has given us.

Practical Ways to Embrace Nourishment as Worship

1. Begin Each Meal with Prayer

A simple prayer of gratitude sets the tone for a mindful and thankful meal. By thanking God, we place our focus on His provision and invite His presence into our daily routines.

2. Choose Foods that Honor God's Creation

Opting for wholesome, natural foods that honor God's creation—fruits, vegetables, grains—reinforces the idea that our bodies deserve the best. These foods sustain our health and reflect the abundance of the earth that God has provided.

3. Slow Down and Savor Each Bite

Eating slowly, without distractions, can be a spiritual discipline. This approach allows us to fully experience the flavors and textures of food and to reflect on God's creativity in the variety of foods He provides.

4. Reflect on the Source of Your Food

Take a moment to consider the journey of your meal, from seed to table. This reflection reminds us that each ingredient is a product of God's handiwork, and many hands contributed to its preparation.

Nourishing the Body, Nourishing the Spirit

Food is both a physical and spiritual gift, one that sustains our bodies and draws us closer to the Creator. Through mindful, grateful eating, we can turn a simple act into a moment of worship, acknowledging God as the source of all nourishment. By taking care of our bodies, we honor Him and live out our calling to treat our lives and resources with reverence.

How Spirituality and Nourishment Can Help to Alleviate Depression

Depression is a complex mental health condition that often requires a holistic approach to healing. While traditional treatment approaches, like therapy and medication, are essential, the integration of spiritual practices—especially mindful nourishment—can play a significant role in supporting mental health. Nourishing the body with purpose and gratitude aligns our physical and spiritual needs, fostering resilience and helping to lift depressive symptoms. This chapter will explore how eating mindfully and honoring the spiritual significance of food, as highlighted in the Bible, can contribute to a holistic strategy for reducing depression.

The Spiritual Significance of Food in Alleviating Depression

1. Nourishment as an Act of Trust and Dependence on God

In times of depression, it's easy to feel isolated and unsupported. However, recognizing food as a gift from God, as presented in Scripture, helps us remember that we are not alone. God's care is present in the simple act of eating, and food becomes a way to experience His love and provision even in difficult times.

> "Therefore do not be anxious, saying, 'What shall we eat?' or 'What shall we drink?' or 'What shall we wear?' For the Gentiles seek after all these things, and your heavenly Father knows that you need them all." – Matthew 6:31-32 (ESV)

This passage reminds us that God is aware of our every need. When we eat with a spirit of trust and gratitude, we reinforce our reliance on Him, which can instill a calming sense of peace and reduce anxiety.

2. Gratitude as a Means to Combat Negativity and Lift Mood

Gratitude has powerful effects on the mind, and it is a potent tool against the negativity associated with depression. When we approach food as a blessing, we cultivate a grateful heart, which in turn has been shown to positively influence mental health. Studies in positive psychology reveal that gratitude exercises improve mood and reduce symptoms of depression. By viewing every meal as an opportunity to give thanks, we transform an everyday habit into a spiritual practice that counters depressive thoughts.

> "Give thanks in all circumstances; for this is the will of God in Christ Jesus for you." – 1 Thessalonians 5:18 (NIV)

Practicing gratitude around meals brings mindfulness to the act of eating and shifts focus from negative to positive thoughts. This mindfulness fosters a greater sense of presence, which is crucial in alleviating symptoms of depression.

3. Healthy, God-Created Foods and Their Role in Healing

Many foods that the Bible encourages us to eat— such as fruits, grains, and honey—are rich in nutrients that can support mental well-being. These foods contain vitamins, minerals, and antioxidants essential for brain health, which can alleviate some of the biological factors contributing to depression.

- Honey is praised throughout Scripture for its nourishing sweetness and restorative properties. It has antioxidant and anti-inflammatory effects, which can benefit mental clarity and energy levels.

- Fruits and vegetables, often symbolizing abundance and God's provision, are filled with vitamins that promote mental wellness. For example, leafy greens are high in folate, a nutrient associated with improved mood and cognitive function.

> "My son, eat honey, for it is good, and the drippings of the honeycomb are sweet to your taste." – Proverbs 24:13 (ESV)

Foods like honey remind us of the richness of God's provision, and consuming them can boost energy and mood, offering a natural lift that can support the healing process from depression.

4. Fasting and Feasting: Spiritual Rhythms of Eating as Tools for Renewal

The Bible encourages both fasting and feasting as spiritual disciplines, rhythms that offer mental and emotional renewal. Fasting can help cultivate a stronger sense of purpose and clarity, while feasting can celebrate God's blessings. For those dealing with depression, these practices can help create structure and a sense of meaning.

- Fasting allows for a time of reflection, rest, and focusing on God, which can be a time for addressing mental burdens and bringing emotional concerns before God.

- Feasting provides a sense of community, joy, and gratitude, helping to lift the spirit through communal celebration and the enjoyment of God's blessings.

> "Then Jesus said to them, 'The days will come when the bridegroom is taken away from them, and then they will fast in those days.'" – Luke 5:35 (ESV)

Fasting offers a purposeful break from daily patterns and encourages spiritual introspection, which can help address underlying thoughts and emotions contributing to depression. In contrast, celebrating with food in joyful moments fosters community, happiness, and gratitude.

Nutrient-Rich Foods as Gifts from God

The Bible describes foods that not only nourish the body but also support emotional wellness. Each meal is a gift that nurtures both body and soul. By understanding food in this way, eating becomes a spiritual act, reminding us of God's loving care.

1. Olive Oil: The Bible refers to olive oil as a symbol of anointing, blessing, and healing. It's a source of healthy fats that support brain health and provide the body with sustained energy.

> "The Lord said to Moses, 'Take the finest spices...with olive oil and make these into a sacred anointing oil.'" – Exodus 30:23-25 (NIV)

Olive oil supports cognitive function and combats inflammation, which has been linked to depressive symptoms. Integrating it into meals as part of a balanced diet can support emotional and physical health.

2. Fish: Often mentioned as a staple in the diet of Jesus and His disciples, fish is rich in omega-3 fatty acids, which have been scientifically linked to improved mental health and reduced depression.

> "They gave him a piece of broiled fish, and he took it and ate before them." – Luke 24:42-43 (NIV)

Including fish in one's diet provides the brain with essential fats, which support mood regulation and may reduce the intensity of depressive symptoms.

3. Bread: Bread is a fundamental symbol of sustenance in the Bible, and Jesus uses it to convey His presence and provision. Bread provides complex carbohydrates, which help stabilize blood sugar and mood, supporting steady energy levels.

> "I am the bread of life. Whoever comes to me will never go hungry, and whoever believes in me will never be thirsty." – John 6:35 (NIV)

Consuming whole grains provides steady energy and supports mental clarity, creating a sense of groundedness and reducing the blood sugar fluctuations that can worsen depression.

Practical Steps to Embrace Spiritual Nourishment

1. Prayerful Eating: Begin each meal with a prayer of gratitude. Recognizing God's provision helps shift focus from depressive thoughts to appreciation, creating a positive framework that uplifts the spirit.

2. Mindful Eating: Practice eating slowly, savoring each bite, and reflecting on the origins and journey of the food. This mindfulness reduces stress and promotes peace, which can alleviate some depressive symptoms.

3. Incorporate Scripture: Integrate Bible verses about God's provision into your meal times. Scriptures on food, sustenance, and thankfulness serve as reminders of God's presence and love.

4. Community Meals: Sharing meals with others builds community, which is essential in battling depression. Studies show that social interaction can significantly reduce depressive symptoms, and gathering around a meal fosters this connection.

Nourishing Body and Spirit

Integrating spirituality into our approach to nutrition fosters a holistic path to healing. Food becomes more than physical sustenance—it becomes a way to connect with God, cultivate gratitude, and nourish the soul. By viewing nourishment as a spiritual discipline, we allow the act of eating to become a source of comfort, healing, and resilience in the face of depression.

Through mindful, prayerful eating and choosing foods that honor God's creation, we align with His wisdom for our well-being, enabling both our bodies and spirits to find renewal.

CHAPTER 05

BUILDING SOCIAL CONNECTIONS

Why Social Support Matters

In the journey to combat depression, social support is one of the most influential and often underappreciated factors. Human beings are social creatures, inherently designed to connect with and support one another. Depression, however, can be profoundly isolating, cutting people off from their support networks and creating a vicious cycle where isolation exacerbates depressive symptoms. Understanding the nature of social support, stress, and mood can help reveal why connections with others are imperative for anyone seeking to overcome depression.

This chapter delves into the nature of social support, explains how stress impacts mental health, and examines how mood is influenced by relationships. Through this exploration, we'll come to see how social support is a powerful tool in the fight against depression, acting as a buffer against stress, enhancing mood, and helping to foster resilience.

What is Social Support?

Social support refers to the psychological and practical assistance received from friends, family, peers, or support networks. It includes emotional, informational, and tangible support that enables individuals to manage life's challenges. Social support can be categorized into three primary forms:

1. Emotional Support: Involves empathy, compassion, love, and encouragement from others. It's the comfort of knowing someone is there to listen and care, which provides relief during stressful situations.

2. Informational Support: Refers to guidance, advice, or information that helps someone manage a particular issue. This support can assist individuals in making decisions, planning actions, or understanding complex situations.

3. Tangible Support: This is practical, hands-on help, like offering assistance with tasks, providing financial aid, or helping in times of crisis.

When people feel supported, they experience a sense of security and belonging that protects them from the harmful effects of stress, especially in the context of depression. Social support doesn't eliminate life's challenges, but it offers a safety net to prevent individuals from being overwhelmed by adversity.

What is Stress?

Stress is the body's reaction to any demand that disrupts its equilibrium. When we perceive a threat or challenge, our bodies undergo physiological and psychological responses, including the release of stress hormones like cortisol and adrenaline. Stress manifests in two forms: acute (short-term) stress, which can be beneficial in moderation, and chronic (long-term) stress, which can harm mental and physical health over time.

When stress becomes chronic, it can contribute to the onset of depression by overwhelming an individual's coping mechanisms. Prolonged exposure to stress hormones weakens the immune system, impairs cognitive function, and diminishes emotional resilience, leading to a greater vulnerability to depression.

Studies in health psychology indicate that high-stress levels without adequate social support can increase the risk of mental health issues, including anxiety and depression. Social support serves as a critical buffer by reducing the intensity of the stress response, helping individuals feel less alone in facing their difficulties.

What is Mood?

Mood is a sustained emotional state that colors an individual's perception of the world. Unlike fleeting emotions, mood is a pervasive, long-lasting affective state that can range from positive to negative. Mood impacts how we interpret events, interact with others, and manage our day-to-day lives.

Moods are influenced by a combination of internal and external factors, including biological rhythms, cognitive patterns, physical health, and social interactions. When someone is in a depressed mood, their thoughts, actions, and outlook become more pessimistic, creating a downward spiral that reinforces negative feelings and perceptions.

Healthy social support can significantly enhance mood by increasing feelings of worthiness and belonging. Positive social interactions release neurotransmitters such as dopamine and oxytocin, often called the "feel-good" chemicals. These neurotransmitters not only improve mood but also foster a sense of calm and well-being, reducing the symptoms of depression.

Social Support as a Buffer Against Stress

Social support acts as a powerful shield against stress. When individuals face challenges alone, they tend to internalize stressors, which can lead to self-criticism, feelings of inadequacy, and despair. In contrast, social support provides a sounding board for thoughts and emotions, allowing individuals to express themselves and gain a different perspective on their challenges. This emotional outlet prevents the build-up of negative feelings and enables individuals to view their situations more objectively.

Research shows that the presence of supportive relationships reduces the physiological impact of stress, as social interactions lower blood pressure, decrease cortisol levels, and promote relaxation. A supportive environment allows people to manage stress more effectively, reducing the risk of depression by fostering resilience and promoting a positive mindset.

How Social Support Lifts Mood

1. Encouragement and Motivation: Supportive people remind us of our strengths and potential, boosting self-esteem and motivation. For someone dealing with depression, this encouragement can counteract feelings of hopelessness and encourage them to take small, positive steps toward healing.

2. Emotional Validation: When friends or family listen empathetically, it helps people feel understood and validated. Being heard alleviates the emotional burden of depression, creating a sense of connection and safety.

3. Shared Activities and Distraction: Engaging in activities with others—such as going for a walk, sharing a meal, or watching a movie—can distract from negative thoughts and introduce moments of joy. These shared experiences foster a positive mood and counteract the isolation that often accompanies depression.

Social Support as an Essential Component in Depression Recovery

The relationship between social support and mental health is well-documented in psychological literature. Studies have shown that people with strong social support systems have lower rates of depression, faster recovery from depressive episodes, and a greater overall sense of well-being. While support systems alone may not cure depression, they provide critical assistance that can make therapeutic interventions more effective. By creating a positive and nurturing environment, social support enhances emotional stability and contributes to a more optimistic outlook.

Why Social Support is Imperative in Overcoming Depression

1. Reduces Feelings of Isolation: Depression often brings about feelings of loneliness and disconnection from others. Having a support network helps break down this isolation, reminding individuals that they are not alone in their struggles.

2. Promotes Accountability: Depression can drain motivation, making it difficult to stick to routines, exercise, or therapy. Supportive friends and family can act as accountability partners, encouraging the individual to stay engaged with their treatment plan.

3. Facilitates Positive Cognitive Restructuring: In the presence of empathetic listeners, individuals are more likely to challenge distorted thoughts and adopt healthier thinking patterns. Social support creates a safe space where individuals can vocalize their thoughts, helping them reframe negative perceptions.

4. Provides Practical Assistance: Depression can make even basic tasks feel overwhelming. Tangible support—such as help with daily responsibilities, transportation to therapy, or meal preparation—relieves some of the burdens of depression, allowing individuals to focus on their healing journey.

5. Encourages Engagement in Positive Activities: Social connections expose individuals to new activities, hobbies, and interests, which can bring moments of joy and satisfaction. Engaging in such activities serves as a distraction from depressive thoughts and encourages the person to rediscover pleasures in life.

Building and Strengthening Social Connections

Establishing and maintaining social connections can be challenging, especially during depressive episodes. However, by setting small, manageable goals, individuals can gradually build a support network that nurtures mental health.

1. Reach Out to Close Friends or Family Members: Begin with people you trust. Share your thoughts and feelings openly, and let them know how they can support you.

2. Engage in Group Activities or Support Groups: Community-based support groups or hobbies can introduce you to new people and build a sense of belonging. Such settings offer opportunities to share experiences and learn from others going through similar struggles.

3. Cultivate Deep Connections Over Superficial Interactions: While having a large circle of acquaintances may offer some social benefits, deep connections are more effective for mental health. Invest in relationships where you can speak honestly and feel genuinely understood.

4. Practice Reciprocal Support: Supporting others can be as healing as receiving support. Volunteering, helping friends, or simply being present for others fosters a sense of purpose and helps redirect attention from personal challenges.

Social Support as a Lifeline in the Journey to Healing

Depression is a complex condition that requires a multi-faceted approach, but social support remains one of the most accessible and impactful tools available. By understanding the nature of social support, stress, and mood, we can see why relationships are essential for well-being and mental health. Strong social connections foster resilience, buffer against stress, and uplift the mood, making them invaluable in overcoming depression.

Investing in social connections is an investment in one's mental health. Whether through family, friends, or community, these bonds form a lifeline that helps individuals navigate the challenges of depression, bringing hope and healing through the power of human connection.

Ways to Connect

Social connection is an essential part of emotional health and a vital support system in managing depression. Building or rebuilding connections can feel challenging, especially during a period of low motivation or energy, yet reaching out to friends, family, and support groups can provide a tremendous source of strength. This chapter provides practical suggestions on how to initiate or deepen connections with loved ones and outlines ways to find and benefit from support groups.

Understanding that connection is a two-way process—giving and receiving—can help foster meaningful relationships that act as a positive force in one's mental health journey.

Reaching Out to Friends and Family

When facing depression, reaching out to those closest to you may feel like a daunting task. Depression often clouds self-perception, leading people to feel as though they are a burden to others. However, friends and family members are often more than willing to offer support if they understand what you're going through. Here are some strategies to initiate contact and communicate your needs to those who care about you.

1. Start Small and Keep It Simple

If you haven't spoken to someone in a while, starting with a simple message can break the ice without pressure. A quick text message, such as "Hey, I just wanted to say hi and see how you're doing," can be a gentle way to reconnect. Keeping it casual and straightforward relieves the pressure of a deep conversation and lets the other person know you're open to contact.

2. Be Honest and Transparent About Your Needs

When reaching out, honesty is crucial. You don't have to disclose everything at once, but sharing a bit about how you're feeling can foster understanding. A simple, "I've been having a tough time lately and could use some company or support," can go a long way. Most friends and family members appreciate directness and are more than willing to lend an ear or offer help if they know what you're going through.

3. Set Up a Regular Check-In

When possible, set up a regular check-in with someone close to you. This could be a weekly coffee date, a short phone call, or even a shared activity like a walk. Regular check-ins create structure, giving you something to look forward to and helping to maintain a sense of connection even during low-energy periods. Having consistent contact with others can ease feelings of isolation and provide stability.

4. Ask for Specific Help

It can be difficult to ask for help, especially when you're feeling vulnerable. However, specific requests make it easier for others to support you. For example, you might ask, "Could we go for a walk together?" or "Would you mind sitting with me while I get some things done around the house?" People who care about you are often grateful to know exactly how they can help and feel reassured that their support is meaningful.

Joining Support Groups

Support groups offer a unique environment where you can connect with people who are experiencing similar challenges. These groups provide a safe space to share your story, listen to others, and gain a sense of belonging. Knowing you're not alone in your struggles can be incredibly comforting, and support groups can be a significant part of building resilience.

1. Identify Your Needs and Preferences

When searching for a support group, consider what you're hoping to gain. Some groups focus on sharing personal stories, while others provide practical coping strategies. Some groups are led by mental health professionals, while others are peer-led. Deciding on your preferences will help you find a group that feels right for you.

2. Online vs. In-Person Groups

Both online and in-person groups have unique advantages. In-person meetings can foster a more personal connection, allowing you to read body language and establish trust within a physical space. However, online groups offer greater flexibility and convenience, especially if you have limited energy or find it challenging to leave home.

Online platforms also offer the advantage of anonymity, which can help ease self-consciousness and allow for more openness. You can explore a variety of groups until you find one that feels comfortable and supportive.

3. Make Use of Community Resources

Many communities have mental health centers, religious organizations, or nonprofit groups that organize support groups. Often, these are free or low-cost resources available to anyone who wants to participate. If you're unsure where to start, ask your healthcare provider, therapist, or local community center for recommendations. Religious communities may also have faith-based support groups, which can integrate spiritual insights alongside mental health support.

4. Share and Listen with Openness

In support groups, an open and non-judgmental mindset is essential. Being open to listening to others' experiences not only provides perspective but can also help reduce feelings of isolation. In sharing your story, you give others the opportunity to relate to you, and in listening to them, you may find commonalities that help you feel less alone in your struggles.

Deepening Connections Through Shared Activities

Activities shared with others can reinforce social bonds and build trust in a natural way, without the need for heavy conversations. Engaging in simple, shared activities can create positive experiences and enhance the joy of companionship.

1. Try Simple Activities Together

A low-stress way to connect is by engaging in simple, everyday activities with friends or family members. Cooking a meal together, going for a nature walk, playing a game, or watching a movie are all examples of activities that can promote bonding. Shared activities offer an opportunity to enjoy each other's company without putting too much pressure on conversation.

2. Incorporate Physical Activity for Added Benefits

Physical activities such as yoga, walking, or playing a sport with others can be particularly beneficial, as they not only foster connection but also provide mental health benefits by releasing endorphins. Joining a walking group or taking a fitness class with friends can add structure to your week and boost your mood.

3. Join Hobby or Interest-Based Groups

Interest-based groups allow you to meet new people in a relaxed setting. Book clubs, art classes, gardening groups, and music groups offer opportunities to interact with others while participating in something you enjoy. These groups can bring a sense of achievement and fulfillment, which are often needed when struggling with depression.

Utilizing Technology to Stay Connected

Technology can be a useful tool in maintaining social connections, especially when meeting in person is not possible. Here are some ways to use technology to enhance social support.

1. Stay in Touch Through Social Media (Mindfully)

Social media can be a double-edged sword when it comes to mental health. However, when used mindfully, it can offer meaningful ways to connect with friends and family members, share your experiences, and receive supportive feedback. Limit your time on social media to avoid overstimulation, and focus on positive interactions that uplift you.

2. Use Video Calls for a More Personal Connection

Video calls can bridge the gap between phone calls and in-person meetings. Seeing someone's face, even through a screen, can create a sense of closeness and ease the feelings of isolation. Regular video calls with friends or family members can maintain intimacy, especially when physical distance makes in-person meetings difficult.

3. Explore Mental Health Apps for Community Support

Some mental health apps offer online community features, where users can connect with others facing similar struggles. These platforms provide a safe space to share, ask for advice, and offer encouragement to others. However, always prioritize reputable apps, preferably those recommended by mental health professionals.

Nurturing Social Connections for Emotional Resilience

Building and nurturing connections may take time, but the rewards are worth the effort. A strong support network can help foster resilience, providing emotional and practical resources when depression feels overwhelming. Social support does not replace professional treatment, but it can enhance its effectiveness, creating a supportive environment that makes recovery more attainable. By reaching out to others, engaging in shared activities, and being open to new social experiences, you can begin to build a web of connections that supports and sustains your mental and emotional well-being.

This journey toward connection is not linear, and it may have ups and downs. But every step taken to strengthen social ties is a step toward a healthier, more connected self. Remember that everyone faces challenges, and seeking support is a natural and courageous part of the healing process.

Faith Communities as a Source of Support

Faith communities—including churches, mosques, temples, and other religious gatherings—serve as powerful sources of emotional and spiritual support. For centuries, these communities have offered comfort, guidance, and a sense of belonging to individuals facing various challenges, including mental health struggles like depression. Faith communities provide not only a spiritual home but also a practical network of support, which can be crucial in times of crisis.

This chapter explores the nature of faith communities, their role in helping alleviate the burdens of depression, and the spiritual support they offer. Using Biblical insights and drawing on expository studies with strong concordance references, we will uncover how faith communities can bring healing, resilience, and a sense of peace.

Understanding Faith Communities

Faith communities are groups of people who gather regularly to worship, pray, and support one another in their spiritual journeys. These communities are often centered around places of worship—churches, mosques, synagogues, temples—and consist of members who share common beliefs and values. While each faith community may vary in its practices and teachings, they are all unified by a sense of devotion to a higher power and a commitment to communal care.

Types of Faith Communities

1. Churches: In Christianity, churches serve as houses of worship where believers gather to pray, listen to sermons, and engage in fellowship. The New Testament describes the

early Christian community as one of unity and support, reflecting the deep bond shared among believers (Acts 2:42-47).

2. Mosques: For Muslims, mosques are places of worship where individuals gather to pray, reflect, and learn together. The Qur'an emphasizes the importance of community and mutual support, with a focus on compassion and care for those in need.

3. Temples: Temples are places of worship for many religions, including Hinduism and Buddhism. Here, individuals come together to practice meditation, offer prayers, and support each other's spiritual growth.

4. Synagogues: In Judaism, synagogues serve as centers for worship, study, and community gatherings, offering a sense of continuity and support.

The Role of Faith Communities in Supporting Mental Health

Faith communities provide significant mental health benefits through fellowship, compassionate care, and opportunities for growth. Depression often isolates individuals, creating a sense of loneliness and despair. Faith communities can bridge this isolation, surrounding individuals with encouragement, prayer, and the reminder that they are not alone.

Fellowship and Belonging

One of the essential elements that faith communities offer is fellowship. This is the shared bond of friendship and unity among believers. In the Bible, fellowship is emphasized as a critical aspect of the early Christian community. Acts 2:42 tells us that "they devoted themselves to the apostles' teaching and the fellowship, to the breaking of bread and the prayers." Fellowship offers both emotional and practical support, helping people feel seen, valued, and understood.

- Galatians 6:2: "Bear one another's burdens, and so fulfill the law of Christ." This verse highlights the importance of mutual support, which is a foundational principle in faith communities. Through fellowship, believers can share in each other's pain and alleviate some of the burdens that depression may bring.

Spiritual Guidance and Counseling

Faith communities often have spiritual leaders—pastors, imams, rabbis—who provide guidance, counseling, and encouragement. In times of depression, receiving support from a trusted spiritual mentor can offer a perspective rooted in faith and hope. Many leaders in these communities are trained in pastoral counseling and understand the emotional and spiritual struggles that can accompany mental health issues. This type of support, combined with Biblical encouragement, can provide a holistic approach to healing.

- Proverbs 11:14: "Where there is no guidance, a people falls, but in an abundance of counselors there is safety." This verse reflects the value of wise counsel in times of difficulty. Seeking guidance from spiritual leaders and members of one's faith community can help individuals navigate their struggles with a sense of direction and hope.

Prayer and Meditation as Spiritual Healing

Prayer and meditation are core practices in many faith communities, providing solace, inner peace, and connection to God. Through prayer, individuals can express their feelings, fears, and hopes, finding comfort in God's presence. Research has shown that prayer and meditation can help reduce stress and increase resilience, making these practices valuable for those experiencing depression.

- Psalm 34:17-18: "When the righteous cry for help, the Lord hears and delivers them out of all their troubles. The Lord is near to the brokenhearted and saves the crushed in spirit." These verses remind believers of God's compassion and closeness to those who are suffering. In faith communities, prayer is seen as a direct line to God, offering peace and strength.

Practical Support Through Faith Communities

Faith communities are also known for their emphasis on charitable acts and providing practical assistance. Many places of worship have support groups, outreach programs, and resources that can help individuals in tangible ways. Depression can make daily tasks and responsibilities feel overwhelming, and having access to a network that can help with practical needs—such as food, companionship, or financial aid—can make a difference.

Support Groups

Many faith communities organize support groups specifically for mental health concerns, addiction, grief, and other life challenges. These groups provide a safe, non-judgmental environment where individuals can share their experiences, receive empathy, and find a sense of unity with others facing similar struggles.

Acts of Service

Service is central to the mission of most faith communities. Churches and other religious organizations often provide meals, visit the sick, and offer financial aid to those in need. These acts of service not only fulfill the Biblical commandment to love one another but also provide relief and support to those who are struggling with depression.

- Matthew 25:35-36: "For I was hungry and you gave me food, I was thirsty and you gave me drink, I was a stranger and you welcomed me, I was naked and you clothed me, I was sick and you visited me, I was in prison and you came to me."

This passage emphasizes the importance of serving those in need, an ethos that many faith communities uphold.

Faith and Resilience in Times of Suffering

Faith communities provide a framework of hope and resilience in times of suffering. Belief in a higher purpose, the promise of eternal peace, and God's unfailing love can be particularly comforting when facing despair. This spiritual perspective allows individuals to place their trust in something greater than themselves, giving them strength to endure and overcome their struggles.

- Romans 8:18: "For I consider that the sufferings of this present time are not worth comparing with the glory that is to be revealed to us." This verse offers hope, encouraging believers to view their current struggles as temporary in light of the eternal peace that faith promises.

Faith communities help individuals connect their suffering to a broader narrative of faith and redemption. This perspective does not diminish the pain of depression but gives it context, allowing believers to see themselves as part of God's plan and purpose.

How Faith Communities Help Alleviate Depression

Faith communities provide a comprehensive support system, combining spiritual, emotional, and practical resources. For many individuals, this network can help alleviate feelings of hopelessness and isolation. Knowing there are people who care deeply and are willing to offer support can make the journey through depression more bearable.

Faith-based gatherings are filled with opportunities for growth and learning, providing a structure of accountability, guidance, and love that can enhance the healing process. Depression may still be a difficult path, but with the support of a compassionate and unified faith community, individuals can find solace, strength, and ultimately, hope.

The Power of Community and Faith

Faith communities embody a sense of connection and compassion that can be crucial for those dealing with depression. By engaging in fellowship, seeking guidance, participating in acts of service, and embracing the healing power of prayer, individuals can find a source of strength and resilience within their spiritual community. As Proverbs 17:17 reminds us, "A friend loves at all times, and a brother is born for a time of adversity."

In the warmth and care of a faith community, individuals can experience healing that addresses the mind, body, and spirit. Through the shared values of love, service, and faith, these communities offer a path not only toward relief from depression but also toward a life enriched with purpose, support, and divine hope.

CHAPTER 06

AVOIDING HARMFUL SUSTANCES

In the journey to manage and overcome depression, avoiding harmful substances is crucial. While alcohol, nicotine, and caffeine are commonly used worldwide, they can significantly impact mood, mental clarity, and overall well-being. For individuals dealing with depression, these substances may seem to offer temporary relief or a quick lift in energy, but the effects are often short-lived, and their use can ultimately worsen depressive symptoms. This chapter explores how each of these substances—alcohol, nicotine, and caffeine—affects mental health and examines evidence supporting the importance of avoiding them as part of a holistic approach to managing depression.

How Alcohol Affects Mental Health

The Immediate Effects of Alcohol

Alcohol is a central nervous system depressant, meaning that it slows down brain activity, leading to temporary feelings of relaxation and reduced inhibition. For some, alcohol may provide a sense of escape or relief from depressive symptoms. However, these effects are fleeting and can quickly lead to a "crash," where feelings of sadness and hopelessness return more strongly.

Alcohol's Impact on Mood and Depression

Research shows that alcohol can worsen depressive symptoms by altering the balance of neurotransmitters in the brain. Neurotransmitters such as serotonin and dopamine are essential for regulating mood and emotions. When alcohol is consumed, it temporarily increases the release of these chemicals, creating a feeling of euphoria or relief. However, as the body processes and eliminates alcohol, these neurotransmitter levels plummet, resulting in mood swings and even depressive episodes.

- Study Evidence: A study published in The Lancet Psychiatry revealed that people with alcohol use disorders are significantly more likely to experience depressive episodes compared to those who do not consume alcohol regularly. Furthermore, individuals who abuse alcohol are at a higher risk of suicidal thoughts and actions, especially during times of withdrawal when depressive symptoms may intensify.

The Vicious Cycle of Alcohol and Depression

People who use alcohol as a coping mechanism may find themselves in a cycle where they feel compelled to drink to alleviate depressive symptoms, only to find that alcohol worsens those very symptoms. This cycle of dependency can lead to increased tolerance and addiction, making it harder to abstain and potentially leading to alcohol use disorder.

- Proverbs 20:1: "Wine is a mocker, strong drink is raging: and whosoever is deceived thereby is not wise." This verse warns against the deceptive allure of alcohol. While it may promise relief, it often leads to anger, conflict, and a deepening of negative emotions.

Nicotine and Its Effect on Depression

Nicotine's Short-Term Mood Boost

Nicotine, commonly ingested through smoking, vaping, or chewing tobacco, is another substance that temporarily stimulates dopamine release in the brain. This release creates a brief sense of pleasure or calm, which is why many people with depression are drawn to nicotine to alleviate symptoms.

However, similar to alcohol, the relief nicotine provides is only temporary. As the body metabolizes nicotine, dopamine levels drop sharply, leaving the user craving more. This craving contributes to a cycle of dependence, which can ultimately increase feelings of anxiety and depression rather than relieve them.

The Long-Term Impact of Nicotine on Mental Health

Over time, regular nicotine use damages various systems in the body, particularly the respiratory and cardiovascular systems. Poor physical health can directly impact mental health, leading to fatigue, low energy, and worsened depressive symptoms. Furthermore, the psychological effects of nicotine dependence, including irritability, anxiety, and withdrawal symptoms, can contribute to emotional distress.

- Study Evidence: A study published in Addictive Behaviors found a strong correlation between nicotine dependence and the severity of depressive symptoms. Smokers with depression experienced more significant mood swings and irritability than non-smokers, indicating that nicotine does not alleviate depression in the long term and may even exacerbate it.

Breaking Free from Nicotine Addiction

Quitting nicotine can lead to withdrawal symptoms, including irritability, mood swings, and even mild depressive symptoms as the brain adjusts to a lack of nicotine. However, these symptoms are temporary, and research indicates that former smokers experience better mental health and reduced depression once they have successfully quit.

- 1 Corinthians 6:19-20: "Do you not know that your body is a temple of the Holy Spirit within you, whom you have from God? You are not your own, for you were bought with a price. So glorify God in your body." This verse encourages believers to honor their physical health as a way of respecting the gift of life from God. Avoiding substances like nicotine, which harm the body and mind, aligns with this teaching.

The Effects of Caffeine on Mood and Anxiety

The Temporary Energy Boost of Caffeine

Caffeine is a stimulant commonly found in coffee, tea, energy drinks, and sodas. For many people, caffeine provides a quick energy boost, improves alertness, and temporarily reduces fatigue. While caffeine may seem like a helpful tool for combating low energy, its effects on mental health, particularly for those struggling with depression and anxiety, are mixed.

Caffeine's Impact on Anxiety and Depression

Caffeine stimulates the release of adrenaline, the "fight-or-flight" hormone, which increases heart rate, blood pressure, and alertness. For individuals prone to anxiety or depression, this can lead to jitteriness, restlessness, and even panic attacks. Furthermore, excessive caffeine consumption can disrupt sleep patterns, and poor sleep quality is strongly linked to depression.

- Study Evidence: Research published in Depression and Anxiety demonstrated that high levels of caffeine intake are associated with increased anxiety and panic disorder. Additionally, caffeine withdrawal symptoms, such as headaches, irritability, and fatigue, can mimic or worsen depressive symptoms in people who are already vulnerable.

Caffeine and the Sleep-Depression Cycle

Caffeine can have a half-life of several hours, meaning it remains in the body for an extended period. Consuming caffeine late in the day can disrupt sleep cycles, contributing to insomnia or poor-quality sleep. Since sleep is essential for mental resilience, this disruption can aggravate depression over time.

- Psalm 127:2: "It is vain for you to rise up early, to sit up late, to eat the bread of sorrows: for so he giveth his beloved sleep." This verse underscores the importance of rest as a gift from God. Consuming substances that interfere with sleep contradicts the principle of honoring the body and mind with rest.

The Benefits of Avoiding Harmful Substances in Managing Depression

Choosing to avoid or limit the intake of alcohol, nicotine, and caffeine can provide both immediate and long-term mental health benefits. By abstaining from these substances, individuals struggling with depression may experience:

- Stabilized Mood: Without the sharp peaks and crashes associated with these substances, mood swings become less frequent, and individuals can maintain a more balanced emotional state.

- Improved Sleep Quality: Sleep is vital for mental health, and avoiding stimulants and depressants helps individuals experience restful, restorative sleep.

- Enhanced Physical Health: Avoiding harmful substances reduces the risk of chronic illnesses and improves overall energy levels, contributing to a healthier mind-body connection.

- Reduced Anxiety: Eliminating caffeine and nicotine can reduce physical symptoms of anxiety, such as jitteriness and rapid heartbeat, helping individuals feel calmer.

Practical Steps for Reducing or Eliminating Harmful Substances

1. Gradual Reduction: Sudden withdrawal from substances like caffeine and nicotine can lead to withdrawal symptoms. Reducing intake gradually can minimize discomfort and make quitting more manageable.

2. Seek Support: Friends, family, support groups, and even faith communities can provide encouragement and accountability during the process.

3. Replace with Healthier Alternatives: Drinking herbal teas, practicing mindfulness, and engaging in physical activities can replace the cravings for these substances.

4. Rely on Prayer and Faith: For individuals with strong spiritual beliefs, prayer and meditation can be powerful tools for coping with cravings and emotional struggles.

Embracing a Healthier Path

Avoiding alcohol, nicotine, and caffeine can significantly contribute to improved mental health and resilience against depression. While these substances may offer temporary relief, their long-term impact often exacerbates the very symptoms they are intended to relieve. By embracing a lifestyle that prioritizes mental clarity, physical health, and spiritual well-being, individuals can cultivate a more balanced and hopeful approach to managing depression.

Faith can be a powerful motivator in this journey, providing strength, accountability, and purpose. When we honor our bodies and minds as gifts from God, we take an active role in our healing process. By choosing to eliminate harmful substances, we move closer to a healthier, more fulfilled life aligned with spiritual values and mental wellness.

Strategies for Avoidance

For individuals striving to manage or overcome depression, reducing dependency on harmful substances like alcohol, nicotine, and caffeine is a fundamental step. Substance dependency can create a vicious cycle that exacerbates symptoms of depression, anxiety, and low energy, making it challenging to achieve stability. This chapter outlines practical, step-by-step strategies to reduce or eliminate dependency on these substances, offering a pathway to clearer thinking, balanced emotions, and improved physical health. By understanding and implementing these steps, individuals can create a healthier foundation for mental well-being.

Step 1: Set Clear Goals and Intentions

The first step in reducing or eliminating harmful substances is to set clear, personal goals for why you want to change your behavior. Having a clear reason for this change, whether it's improved mental health, better physical health, spiritual growth, or a combination, can be a powerful motivator.

1. Identify Your Motivation: Write down why you want to reduce or quit using these substances. Keeping your motivation visible can help you stay focused during challenging moments.

2. Set Specific Goals: Decide on a timeline and whether you plan to gradually reduce or completely eliminate your use. Start with a short-term goal, like reducing intake by a certain amount each week, and set a long-term goal for complete elimination if that is your aim.

Step 2: Educate Yourself on the Effects

Understanding how alcohol, nicotine, and caffeine affect your body and mind can strengthen your resolve. Research and knowledge give you insight into how these substances are impacting your mood, sleep, and overall mental health.

1. Research the Physical and Mental Impact: Learn about the short-term and long-term effects of each substance on mental health. Knowing how they increase depressive symptoms, disrupt sleep, and elevate anxiety can reinforce the decision to cut back.

2. Recognize Triggers and Risks: Be aware of situations or emotional states that lead you to use these substances, such as stress, social events, or feelings of

loneliness. Understanding triggers helps you develop proactive strategies to avoid dependency.

Step 3: Create a Gradual Reduction Plan

A gradual reduction plan is often more sustainable and comfortable than attempting to quit cold turkey, especially with substances like caffeine and nicotine, where withdrawal symptoms can be intense.

1. Reduce Incrementally: Set specific, measurable reductions in your intake over time. For instance, reduce your coffee intake by one cup per day, cut down alcohol consumption to a few times per week, or reduce the number of cigarettes you smoke daily.

2. Track Your Progress: Keep a log of how much you consume daily. This record not only helps you see your progress but also provides encouragement as you notice your intake declining.

3. Replace with Healthier Habits: Find alternatives for the behaviors associated with substance use, like drinking herbal teas instead of coffee, chewing gum or snacking instead of smoking, or drinking flavored sparkling water instead of alcohol.

Step 4: Build a Support System

Having a support system can make a significant difference in maintaining your resolve, especially during moments of temptation or stress.

1. Tell Close Friends and Family: Let those you trust know about your goals. They can offer encouragement and accountability.

2. Join a Support Group: Consider joining a group for people working on similar goals, whether in-person or online. Groups like Alcoholics Anonymous (AA), Nicotine Anonymous, or general mental health support groups can provide valuable shared experiences and coping strategies.

3. Lean on Spiritual Community: Faith communities such as churches, mosques, or meditation groups can offer support and guidance, helping you find encouragement from people who share your spiritual or moral values.

Step 5: Substitute with Positive Activities

Substituting harmful substances with positive activities provides new, healthier ways to cope with stress, boredom, or emotions that might otherwise trigger substance use.

1. Exercise Regularly: Physical activity is a proven mood booster and can alleviate some of the stress or low energy that might lead to substance use. Activities like walking, jogging, swimming, and yoga help reduce cravings by naturally releasing endorphins.

2. Practice Mindfulness and Relaxation Techniques: Techniques like meditation, deep breathing exercises, or

journaling can help manage stress and anxiety, which are often triggers for substance use.

3. Engage in Hobbies: Rediscover hobbies that don't involve substances, such as cooking, reading, painting, or gardening. These activities provide joy and relaxation without relying on substances for emotional relief.

Step 6: Create New Routines and Environments

Breaking free from substance use often involves changing routines or environments associated with consumption.

1. Avoid High-Risk Situations: Identify situations where you are most likely to use substances and take steps to avoid or minimize these triggers. For example, if you associate smoking with breaks at work, find alternative activities for those times.

2. Rearrange Your Environment: Make adjustments to your surroundings to reduce the accessibility of harmful substances. Keep alcohol, cigarettes, or coffee out of immediate reach, and replace them with healthier options like water, herbal teas, or nutritious snacks.

3. Develop New Rituals: Replace rituals associated with substance use with new, positive rituals. If you're used to unwinding with alcohol after work, create a new evening ritual that includes reading, a bath, or a non-caffeinated tea.

Step 7: Manage Withdrawal Symptoms

For some, reducing or quitting substances can lead to withdrawal symptoms. Being prepared for this possibility helps you handle the experience with patience and perseverance.

1. Recognize Possible Symptoms: Know that symptoms like headaches, irritability, fatigue, and cravings may arise. These symptoms are usually temporary and will lessen over time as your body adjusts.

2. Use Healthy Coping Mechanisms: When withdrawal symptoms occur, use healthy coping mechanisms like exercise, hydration, or relaxation techniques. Staying physically active and hydrated can alleviate symptoms like headaches and fatigue.

3. Stay Consistent: Withdrawal symptoms can be challenging, but consistency is key. Remind yourself that these discomforts are temporary and that they will pass as your body heals and adjusts to life without these substances.

Step 8: Practice Self-Compassion

Quitting or reducing harmful substances can be a challenging process, and setbacks may occur. Practicing self-compassion can help you stay resilient during difficult moments.

1. Be Kind to Yourself: Understand that change is a journey, and it's normal to experience difficulties. Instead of judging yourself for slip-ups, focus on your overall progress.

2. Celebrate Small Wins: Every step in the right direction, no matter how small, is a success. Reward yourself for milestones achieved, like going a day, a week, or a month with reduced or zero intake.

3. Reflect on Your Motivation: Regularly remind yourself of your reasons for making this change, and focus on the positive impact it will have on your life. Keeping a journal of your progress and experiences can provide motivation and clarity.

Step 9: Seek Professional Help if Needed

For some individuals, quitting or reducing harmful substances might require additional support from healthcare professionals.

1. Consider Counseling or Therapy: Working with a therapist or counselor can provide valuable insights and support. Techniques like Cognitive Behavioral Therapy (CBT) can help address underlying emotional triggers for substance use.

2. Explore Medical Assistance: In cases of severe addiction, medication or treatment programs can help reduce cravings and manage withdrawal symptoms. Consult with a healthcare provider to explore the best options for you.

3. Look into Faith-Based Counseling: Some faith-based organizations offer counseling that integrates spiritual guidance with psychological support, which can be beneficial if spirituality is an essential part of your journey.

Step 10: Maintain Your Progress

The final step is maintaining your progress over the long term. Consistency and commitment are essential for sustaining a substance-free lifestyle and achieving lasting mental health benefits.

1. Establish Long-Term Goals: Set ongoing goals to reinforce your decision to live without harmful substances, such as increasing physical activity, deepening social connections, or furthering spiritual practices.

2. Regularly Review Your Progress: Periodically assess your journey, noting how far you've come and the positive changes you've experienced.

3. Reinforce Positive Habits: Keep practicing the healthy habits you've established, and continue to find new ways to care for your mind and body. Surround yourself with positive influences and activities that support your well-being.

Reducing dependency on harmful substances can have a transformative impact on mental health and overall quality of life. This journey, though challenging, is a step toward achieving a stable, balanced, and joyful life free from the cycles that can worsen depression. By setting clear goals, building a support system, substituting with positive activities, and managing withdrawal symptoms, you can cultivate a healthier lifestyle. With faith, self-compassion, and consistent effort, this journey can not only reduce depression but also empower you to thrive with renewed strength and clarity.

A Theological Perspective on Sobriety and Purity

In many religious traditions, the concepts of sobriety and purity are deeply tied to faith, self-respect, and a commitment to treating the body as a sacred vessel. The Bible, in particular, offers rich teachings on these themes, encouraging believers to pursue a life of restraint, self-control, and reverence for the body as a temple of the Holy Spirit. In this chapter, we explore the theological grounding for sobriety and purity, examining how these practices can offer a pathway to healing, peace, and mental well-being, particularly in managing or alleviating depression.

By drawing on Scripture and theological interpretations, this chapter shows how sobriety and purity are not merely abstentions from harmful substances but are, more profoundly, acts of faith and worship. Through this lens, we will see how living in alignment with these principles can reduce the burden of depression by fostering a stronger, faith-centered identity and sense of purpose.

1. The Body as a Temple of the Holy Spirit

A foundational concept in Christian theology is the belief that the body is a temple for God's Spirit. Paul emphasizes this in 1 Corinthians 6:19-20, where he writes, "Do you not know that your bodies are temples of the Holy Spirit, who is in you, whom you have received from God? You are not your own; you were bought at a price. Therefore honor God with your bodies." This passage reveals several key insights into the Christian perspective on sobriety and purity.

- Temples of the Spirit: Recognizing the body as a temple implies that it is a sacred space. Just as a physical temple is kept clean and respected, so too should we care for our bodies. Sobriety and purity, then, are acts of reverence for this divine gift.

- Self Control as Honor: The call to "honor God with your bodies" suggests that self-control is an act of worship. By abstaining from substances that harm the body or impair the mind, believers show respect for themselves and gratitude toward God.

This teaching aligns well with psychological principles of self-respect and self-care, both of which are essential in managing depression. By reframing sobriety as an act of reverence, individuals may find greater motivation and purpose in their efforts to remain substance-free, which in turn can help alleviate depressive symptoms.

2. The Role of Sobriety in Spiritual Clarity

In the Bible, sobriety is closely linked with maintaining spiritual clarity and connection with God. In 1 Peter 5:8, believers are urged to "be alert and of sober mind. Your enemy the devil prowls around like a roaring lion looking for someone to devour." This verse underscores the importance of mental clarity in the face of spiritual trials and temptations.

- Clarity of Mind: Sobriety supports mental clarity, which allows individuals to remain spiritually vigilant. Substances that impair judgment or dull the senses can cloud one's relationship with God and make it harder to resist temptation.

- Avoiding Spiritual Vulnerability: This verse also emphasizes the vulnerability that arises from intoxication. By remaining sober, believers are better equipped to withstand spiritual challenges, which can include the temptations of despair, hopelessness, and depression.

From a mental health perspective, maintaining a sober mind helps protect against impulsive decisions, improves emotional regulation, and enhances one's ability to process emotions constructively. These benefits directly support mental resilience, which is critical for managing depression.

3. The Call to Purity and Holiness

Purity is another essential element in the theological perspective on sobriety. The Bible frequently associates purity with holiness, suggesting that a life of purity reflects one's commitment to God and spiritual wholeness. In Matthew 5:8, Jesus says, "Blessed are the pure in heart, for they will see God."

- Pursuit of Holiness: Purity is not merely about avoiding physical defilement; it encompasses the mind and soul. Purity in thought and action helps believers align with God's will, reducing inner conflicts and fostering inner peace.

- Seeing God through Purity: Jesus' promise that the pure "will see God" suggests that purity allows for a closer connection with the divine. This spiritual closeness can bring a sense of hope and purpose, which is essential for those struggling with depression.

For individuals experiencing depression, the pursuit of purity can be empowering. Striving for purity encourages positive behaviors, such as self-compassion, forgiveness, and discipline, all of which contribute to a more stable mental and emotional state.

4. Practicing Self-Control as a Fruit of the Spirit

The Bible also lists self-control as a "fruit of the Spirit," emphasizing its significance in the Christian life. In Galatians 5:22-23, Paul writes, "But the fruit of the Spirit is love, joy, peace, forbearance, kindness, goodness, faithfulness, gentleness and self-control. Against such things there is no law."

- Self-Control as a Divine Quality: Self-control is more than a personal virtue; it is a quality that reflects the presence of the Holy Spirit in one's life. Practicing self-control in relation to substances is a way to honor this divine influence.

- Support for Emotional Regulation: Self-control aids in managing impulses, reducing the risk of turning to substances as a coping mechanism. This emotional regulation is essential for individuals working through depression, as it helps prevent dependency on harmful substances for temporary relief.

Cultivating self-control as a fruit of the Spirit provides a spiritual foundation for reducing or eliminating substance use, helping individuals find peace and stability in their journey toward mental wellness.

5. Nourishing the Body as an Act of Gratitude

Another dimension of sobriety and purity is caring for the body as an act of gratitude toward God. In 1 Corinthians 10:31, Paul writes, "So whether you eat or drink or whatever you do, do it all for the glory of God." This teaching encourages believers to be mindful of what they consume, seeing nourishment as an opportunity to honor God.

- Mindful Consumption: Choosing foods and drinks that nourish the body honors God and reinforces self-respect. Conversely, consuming harmful substances dishonors the body, creating physical and mental burdens that can lead to depression.

- Gratitude as Healing: Approaching sobriety from a place of gratitude, rather than restriction, can be transformative. When individuals view their bodies as gifts, they may feel inspired to make healthier choices that promote mental and physical well-being.

Practicing gratitude has been shown to reduce depressive symptoms by promoting a positive outlook and a focus on the present. By viewing sobriety as a form of gratitude, individuals can strengthen their faith and resilience against depression.

6. Seeking Healing through Faith

The Bible offers hope for those struggling with suffering, reminding believers that God is a source of healing and restoration. In Psalm 34:17-18, it is written, "The righteous cry out, and the Lord hears them; he delivers them from all their troubles. The Lord is close to the brokenhearted and saves those who are crushed in spirit."

- Faith in God's Healing: This verse offers comfort, suggesting that God is near to those who are struggling and willing to deliver them from suffering. For individuals battling depression, this promise of divine support can provide hope and strength.

- Turning to God in Times of Weakness: By seeking healing through faith rather than harmful substances, individuals can find peace and comfort that go beyond temporary relief. This reliance on faith can lead to a more enduring sense of purpose and well-being.

Understanding that God is near to the "crushed in spirit" gives individuals the assurance that they are not alone in their struggle. This sense of spiritual support can help reduce feelings of isolation and despair, fostering resilience and mental stability.

Sobriety and Purity as Pathways to Peace

In the Christian faith, sobriety and purity are not merely physical practices but deeply spiritual commitments. These principles encourage believers to honor their bodies, pursue clarity and self-control, and find healing through faith. By aligning one's actions with these teachings, individuals can cultivate a life of purpose, inner peace, and resilience against depression.

For those experiencing depression, the journey toward sobriety and purity offers more than physical health benefits—it provides a spiritual foundation for recovery. By treating the body as a temple, fostering spiritual clarity, practicing self-control, and expressing gratitude, believers can draw closer to God and find comfort in His presence. In this way, sobriety and purity become not only acts of faith but also essential tools for mental and emotional healing, leading to a fuller, more resilient life.

CHAPTER 07

PRACTICING PATIENCE WITH LIFE DECISION

In times of emotional distress, especially during depression, patience can be one of the most challenging yet crucial virtues to practice. Depression can cloud judgment, reduce self-confidence, and increase feelings of hopelessness, leading individuals to make hasty or unwise decisions. This chapter explores why timing is essential when it comes to making significant life choices, especially during periods of depression. We will also examine psychological and practical evidence supporting the importance of patience, offering strategies to help individuals navigate their life decisions thoughtfully and carefully.

1. The Impact of Depression on Decision-Making

Depression often affects cognitive functioning, distorting one's perception of self and the future. Research shows that depression can impair judgment, decision-making, and problem-solving skills, often leading to decisions that one might later regret.

- Impaired Judgment: Depression can cause cognitive biases that make everything seem negative. People with depression are more likely to experience cognitive distortions, such as "catastrophizing" or "black-and-white thinking," which can lead to impulsive, emotionally driven decisions.

- Negative Self-Perception: Depression often lowers self-esteem, making individuals more likely to undervalue their worth or capabilities. This self-doubt can prompt them to make decisions from a place of insecurity, such as settling for less in relationships, jobs, or personal goals.

- Sense of Urgency: Depression often makes individuals feel as if they must make immediate changes to escape their current suffering. This sense of urgency can pressure them into making major life changes — such as quitting a job, moving to a new place, or ending a relationship — without fully considering the consequences.

A study published in the Journal of Affective Disorders highlights how individuals with depression are more prone to making hasty, short-sighted decisions compared to those without depressive symptoms. This is due, in part, to altered brain functioning in regions associated with long-term planning and impulse control. Understanding the effects of depression on decision-making can empower individuals to be patient with themselves and wait until they are in a more balanced emotional state to make life-altering choices.

2. Timing as a Tool for Better Outcomes

Practicing patience in decision-making can serve as a safeguard against regret and promote healthier choices. When individuals allow themselves time to process their emotions and consider their options objectively, they are more likely to make decisions aligned with their long-term well-being.

- Allowing Emotions to Settle: Emotions, particularly intense negative ones, can cloud judgment. Taking time to allow emotions to settle helps to see the situation with greater clarity.

- Gaining Perspective: Decisions made in haste are often reactionary and may not reflect what one truly wants or needs. By delaying decisions, individuals can gain new perspectives or insights that lead to wiser choices.

- Testing Decision Validity: If a decision feels right even after a period of waiting, it is more likely to be a sound decision. Practicing patience allows time to test the "staying power" of a decision and to explore how one might feel about it in different emotional states.

Waiting until depressive symptoms have eased can lead to more balanced and fulfilling decisions. Studies in Psychology and Aging found that delayed decision-making often leads to greater life satisfaction because individuals take more time to consider options fully, and as a result, feel more at peace with their decisions.

3. Strategies for Practicing Patience in Life Decisions

While patience is easier said than done, especially when one is struggling with depressive symptoms, certain strategies can help cultivate this valuable skill.

a. Pause and Reflect

When faced with an important decision, pause and take a step back. Allow yourself time to reflect on the situation without immediate action. Ask yourself:

- How might I feel about this decision if my mood were different?

- What are the potential long-term effects of this choice?

- Could waiting a bit longer lead to a better outcome?

Writing down reflections can also help clarify thoughts and reduce impulsivity.

b. Seek Support from Trusted Individuals

Depression can create a sense of isolation, but seeking advice from trusted friends, family members, or mental health professionals can help ground your decision-making. Others may provide perspectives that depression might be obscuring.

- Discuss Options: Sharing your thoughts and feelings with others can prevent decisions from being made in a vacuum. Loved ones can help you see the bigger picture and may offer alternatives that hadn't occurred to you.

- Gaining Insight from Objectivity: Those who care about you but are not directly affected by your decisions can offer a more objective view. They may notice patterns in your choices or remind you of past decisions made during similar emotional states.

c. Use Visualization and Scenario Planning

Visualizing potential outcomes of each option can help individuals weigh the pros and cons more effectively. Scenario planning involves imagining how one might feel six months or a year after making the decision.

- Pros and Cons List: A classic technique that allows individuals to see the potential consequences of their choices more clearly.

- Future Self Reflection: Imagining how the decision might impact your future self can help build patience, encouraging choices that are beneficial in the long term.

A 2020 study in Frontiers in Psychology demonstrated that individuals who practiced visualization techniques reported greater confidence in their decisions and less regret over time, even if they faced unexpected outcomes.

d. Avoid "All-or-Nothing" Thinking

Depression can lead to black-and-white thinking, where situations are viewed as all good or all bad. Recognizing this pattern and challenging it can create room for more nuanced and thoughtful decision-making.

- Consider Middle Paths: Instead of making a drastic decision, explore smaller, manageable changes that might offer relief without risking significant disruption.

- Practice Flexibility: Allow yourself the freedom to modify your choices based on how you feel over time, rather than feeling locked into a single, irreversible course of action.

4. Biblical Insights on Patience and Waiting

The Bible offers wisdom on the importance of patience, especially when making life decisions. One notable passage is found in Proverbs 19:2, which warns, "Desire without knowledge is not good — how much more will hasty feet miss the way!" This verse highlights the importance of knowledge and wisdom in decision-making, urging believers to avoid acting out of impulse.

"Be Still and Know that I am God" (Psalm 46:10)

This verse serves as a reminder that in times of distress, believers can find peace in trusting God's timing. By waiting on God, individuals are encouraged to seek divine guidance and resist acting from a place of fear or desperation.

- Spiritual Anchoring: Practicing patience in decision-making can help individuals deepen their relationship with God, finding comfort in His sovereignty and guidance.

- Acceptance of Delayed Gratification: The Christian faith teaches that true fulfillment often requires waiting and trusting in God's timing. This perspective can help mitigate the need for immediate solutions, providing hope and reassurance.

"But those who wait on the Lord shall renew their strength" (Isaiah 40:31)

This passage offers hope to those enduring hardship, encouraging them to wait upon the Lord for renewed strength. For individuals struggling with depression, this promise provides assurance that patience can lead to renewal and clarity.

- Renewal through Faith: Waiting on the Lord can bring a sense of spiritual renewal, alleviating the urgency that often accompanies depressive thoughts.

- Strength for the Journey: Trusting in God's timing allows individuals to gather strength rather than rushing into potentially harmful decisions, knowing that their patience will be rewarded.

The Value of Patience in the Healing Process

Practicing patience in decision-making is more than an act of caution; it is a powerful form of self-respect and a means of seeking true alignment with one's values and goals. By refraining from making hasty decisions during periods of depression, individuals can protect themselves from unintended consequences and gain the clarity needed to make fulfilling choices. The journey to healing and resilience, while challenging, can be strengthened by embracing patience and trusting in the timing that brings inner peace and wisdom.

Tips for Delaying Major Decisions

How to Practice Patience and Wait Until Mental Clarity Returns

Making major life decisions while in a state of emotional turmoil, especially during depression, can lead to outcomes that may not align with long-term goals and well-being. Depression can cloud judgment and create an urgency to escape negative feelings, leading to impulsive choices. This chapter focuses on the importance of practicing patience and waiting until mental clarity returns before making life-altering decisions. We will explore practical tips for exercising patience, what it means to achieve mental clarity, and how the practice of patience can ultimately help reduce the intensity of depression.

1. Understanding Patience and Its Benefits

Patience is the ability to wait calmly and tolerate delay without acting impulsively or out of frustration. It is a skill that allows people to pause, reflect, and make thoughtful choices, especially in challenging times. Patience is often viewed as a virtue because it enables individuals to cope with adversity, reduce stress, and make sound decisions based on rational thinking rather than reactive emotions.

In the context of mental health, patience can be especially valuable. Depression can make it hard to see past present struggles, and patience offers the breathing room needed to let challenging emotions pass without forcing immediate, potentially regrettable actions.

Benefits of Practicing Patience During Depression:

- Enhanced Decision-Making: With patience, individuals can avoid impulsive decisions, which may lead to regret or harm.

- Reduced Stress: Being patient lowers the immediate stress and anxiety that often accompany decision-making.

- Improved Emotional Regulation: Patience encourages one to cope with emotions rather than escape them, fostering resilience.

- Better Outcomes: Pausing allows one to choose actions that are truly aligned with long-term goals and values, leading to more fulfilling results.

2. Achieving Mental Clarity

Mental clarity is a state of mind where one's thoughts are organized, focused, and free from overwhelming emotions. It involves seeing situations objectively, without the distortion of emotional turbulence, particularly the distortions that often accompany depression, such as negative thinking and self-doubt. Mental clarity provides the clear-headedness needed to make well-informed, balanced choices that reflect true desires and values.

When struggling with depression, achieving mental clarity can be challenging, but it is not impossible. Recognizing and respecting one's need for clarity can prevent actions driven by temporary emotions.

How Mental Clarity Helps in Decision-Making:

- Enables Objective Thinking: Clarity allows a person to assess the pros and cons of a decision without the bias of strong emotions.

- Increases Self-Confidence: Making decisions with a clear mind boosts confidence, as individuals are less likely to second-guess themselves.

- Promotes Peace of Mind: Knowing a decision was made thoughtfully can help ease any regrets or concerns about potential outcomes.

3. Practical Tips for Delaying Major Decisions

Here are some strategies to help cultivate patience and wait for mental clarity before making significant decisions. These tips can serve as a guide to avoid impulsive choices and allow for better mental health management in the face of depression.

Tip 1: Set a Waiting Period

One way to prevent impulsive decisions is to set a self-imposed waiting period before taking any action. For example, commit to waiting at least two weeks before making a decision. This break allows emotions to settle and gives time for rational thinking to resurface.

- How It Helps: The waiting period serves as a buffer between the emotional urge and the action, reducing the chance of reactive choices.

- Practical Steps: When a decision feels urgent, write it down and set a date to revisit it in two weeks. This simple practice can prevent emotionally driven decisions and create a habit of delayed gratification.

Tip 2: Break Down Decisions into Smaller Steps

Big decisions can feel overwhelming, particularly during periods of depression. Instead of trying to address the entire issue at once, break it down into smaller, manageable steps. This gradual approach helps avoid drastic actions and encourages patience.

- How It Helps: By focusing on one small step at a time, the urgency to make a final decision diminishes, and it becomes easier to think clearly.

- Practical Steps: For example, if contemplating a job change, start with smaller tasks, such as researching job options or updating a resume. This incremental approach allows time to evaluate each step thoughtfully.

Tip 3: Use a Decision-Making Journal

Keeping a journal specifically for decision-making can be a powerful tool for achieving mental clarity. By writing down the pros, cons, and emotional aspects of a choice, one can see their thoughts in a structured format.

- How It Helps: Journaling enables self-reflection, making it easier to identify underlying emotions and assumptions influencing decisions.

- Practical Steps: Dedicate a few minutes daily to write about decisions weighing on your mind. Record your emotions, fears, hopes, and practical considerations. Revisiting these entries over time can provide valuable insights and help prevent rushed decisions.

Tip 4: Talk to a Trusted Friend or Counselor

Discussing potential decisions with a trusted friend, family member, or mental health counselor can offer a fresh perspective. Often, another person can provide objective insights that are hard to see from within a depressed mindset.

- How It Helps: Talking it out helps reduce feelings of isolation and gives feedback that may lead to better-informed choices.

- Practical Steps: Choose someone who is supportive and non-judgmental. Share your thoughts and ask for feedback on whether the decision seems balanced or influenced by current emotions.

Tip 5: Engage in Mindfulness or Meditation

Practices like mindfulness and meditation can help reduce stress, increase patience, and improve mental clarity. These practices promote a sense of calm and centeredness, which are essential for clear decision-making.

- How It Helps: Mindfulness reduces reactive thinking, helping you pause and consider choices without emotional bias.

- Practical Steps: Begin with short, guided meditation sessions or mindfulness exercises focused on breathing. These practices encourage staying present rather than rushing into future actions, fostering patience and resilience.

Tip 6: Reflect on Long-Term Goals

Depression can make it hard to see beyond immediate struggles, but taking time to reflect on long-term goals can provide a stabilizing influence on decision-making. Ask yourself if the choice aligns with your core values and long-term aspirations.

- How It Helps: Focusing on long-term goals creates a sense of direction and purpose, making it easier to avoid decisions that only address temporary discomfort.

- Practical Steps: Write down three to five long-term goals and revisit them when making decisions. This reflection can help you stay anchored in your values rather than letting temporary emotions dictate your choices.

Tip 7: Practice Self-Compassion

Being patient with oneself is essential in managing depression. Self-compassion involves treating oneself with kindness rather than criticism. Recognize that delaying decisions does not indicate failure but reflects a commitment to well-being.

- How It Helps: Self-compassion reduces pressure and allows individuals to accept that waiting is sometimes necessary for mental health.

- Practical Steps: When feeling impatient or critical, remind yourself of the value of patience and the importance of mental clarity. Treat yourself with the same understanding and grace you would offer a close friend facing similar struggles.

4. How Patience Can Help Reduce Depression

Patience helps in reducing the stress and anxiety that come from feeling pressured to act immediately. By allowing oneself time to think, individuals can avoid impulsive actions that may worsen depression. Patience also promotes emotional resilience by encouraging one to sit with feelings rather than escape them through hasty decisions.

Reducing Cognitive Overload: Depression often brings a flood of negative thoughts. Patience helps reduce this overload by encouraging one to focus on one thing at a time, lowering mental stress.

Building Emotional Resilience: Practicing patience allows individuals to handle difficult emotions more effectively. This resilience is crucial for managing depression, as it fosters the belief that difficult emotions will pass without needing immediate action.

The ability to delay major decisions until mental clarity returns is a skill that can enhance life satisfaction and support the journey toward mental health recovery. Practicing patience empowers individuals to make choices that reflect true desires and values rather than temporary emotions. By adopting strategies such as setting a waiting period, journaling, talking to trusted individuals, and reflecting on long-term goals, individuals can develop patience as a supportive tool for navigating life's challenges.

Ultimately, patience nurtures self-compassion and resilience, helping individuals to reduce the intensity of depressive symptoms and improve their overall quality of life.

Spiritual Perspectives on Timing and Patience

Insights on the Importance of Trusting Divine Timing and Surrendering One's Worries

One of the most profound spiritual practices in facing life's challenges, especially in moments of struggle with mental health, is learning to trust divine timing and surrendering worries to God. This chapter explores how trusting in God's timing and letting go of anxiety can bring peace, reduce depression, and offer a spiritual pathway to healing. Through an exploration of biblical teachings, we will see how the wisdom of scripture encourages us to rely on God's perfect timing, exercise patience, and find comfort in His guidance.

1. Understanding Divine Timing and Patience

In moments of difficulty, it is natural to desire immediate relief or resolution. However, the Bible teaches that God's timing, also known as kairos (Strong's G2540), is divinely orchestrated and often operates beyond our understanding. According to Ecclesiastes 3:1, "To everything there is a season, and a time to every purpose under the heaven" (KJV). This verse reminds us that every aspect of our lives is part of a divine order, unfolding according to God's plan.

Patience, often translated from the Greek makrothumia (Strong's G3115), is emphasized throughout scripture as a virtue that helps us endure and trust that God is working even when we do not immediately see His hand. Practicing patience requires faith in God's wisdom and belief that He is guiding each of us toward a purpose that aligns with His will.

Benefits of Trusting Divine Timing in Overcoming Depression

1. Relieves Pressure for Immediate Solutions: Trusting God's timing helps release the pressure to find instant relief or make impulsive changes, which can often worsen depression.

2. Builds Emotional Resilience: By surrendering to God's timeline, we build resilience, knowing that each challenge we face is part of our spiritual growth.

3. Provides a Sense of Purpose: Believing in divine timing allows us to see each season as an opportunity to grow and deepen our relationship with God, which can alleviate the feelings of purposelessness often associated with depression.

2. Surrendering Worries to God

Anxiety and depression often stem from carrying burdens too heavy to bear alone. Jesus invites us to surrender our worries to Him: "Come unto me, all ye that labor and are heavy laden, and I will give you rest" (Matthew 11:28, KJV).

In this promise, Jesus reassures us that we do not have to carry our struggles alone. By surrendering our anxieties to God, we can experience a peace that surpasses understanding, as described in Philippians 4:6-7: "Be anxious for nothing, but in everything by prayer and supplication, with thanksgiving, let your requests be made known to God. And the peace of God, which surpasses all understanding, will guard your hearts and minds through Christ Jesus."

What Does Surrender Mean?

Surrendering to God does not mean giving up on finding solutions to our problems but rather entrusting them into God's hands. It involves recognizing that God's wisdom is greater than ours and that He knows what is best for us. This form of surrender helps alleviate the sense of responsibility for controlling every outcome, allowing us to rest in God's promises and experience relief from depressive thoughts.

How Surrendering Worries to God Can Reduce Depression

1. Promotes Peace: When we release our burdens to God, we experience a calming peace that diminishes feelings of stress and anxiety.

2. Encourages Trust: Surrender builds our trust in God's faithfulness, reminding us that He will guide us through every trial.

3. Reduces Feelings of Isolation: Surrendering our worries to God creates a sense of companionship, knowing we are not alone in our struggles.

3. Key Bible Verses on Trusting God's Timing and Surrender

Psalm 37:7 – Rest in the Lord and Wait Patiently

"Rest in the Lord, and wait patiently for him: fret not thyself because of him who prospereth in his way, because of the man who bringeth wicked devices to pass" (Psalm 37:7, KJV).

In this verse, rest (damam in Hebrew, Strong's H1826) signifies a quiet trust and stillness in the presence of God. Waiting patiently is a call to faith, reminding us to remain calm and trust that God is in control, even when others may seem to be succeeding while we struggle. Resting in God encourages us to let go of comparison and jealousy, which can exacerbate depression, and focus instead on His faithfulness.

Proverbs 3:5-6 – Trust in the Lord with All Your Heart

"Trust in the Lord with all thine heart; and lean not unto thine own understanding. In all thy ways acknowledge him, and he shall direct thy paths" (Proverbs 3:5-6, KJV).

This passage calls us to release control and acknowledge that our understanding is limited compared to God's omniscience. The phrase "he shall direct thy paths" is a powerful reminder that God will guide us if we place our trust in Him. By releasing the need to understand every situation, we allow God's peace to take root, which can alleviate depressive symptoms related to overthinking and fear.

Isaiah 40:31 – Renewed Strength Through Waiting on the Lord

"But they that wait upon the Lord shall renew their strength; they shall mount up with wings as eagles; they shall run, and not be weary; and they shall walk, and not faint" (Isaiah 40:31, KJV).

This verse reinforces the transformative power of trusting in God's timing. Waiting upon the Lord implies patience and active hope, trusting that God will empower and renew us. In the context of depression, this verse is a promise that God's strength is available to those who wait on Him, providing relief from feelings of fatigue and discouragement.

Jeremiah 29:11 – Plans to Prosper and Not Harm

"For I know the thoughts that I think toward you, saith the Lord, thoughts of peace, and not of evil, to give you an expected end" (Jeremiah 29:11, KJV).

Jeremiah reminds us that God's plans are rooted in love and are designed for our ultimate good. When depression causes feelings of hopelessness, this verse serves as an anchor, reminding us that God's plans are peaceful and purposeful. Even when the future feels uncertain, trusting in God's promises can help us endure the present with hope.

4. Cultivating Patience and Surrender in Daily Life

Here are practical ways to cultivate patience and surrender, allowing us to better trust God's timing and alleviate symptoms of depression.

Step 1: Start Each Day with Prayer and Reflection

Begin each day by surrendering your worries to God through prayer. By consciously releasing your concerns to Him, you invite God's peace into your heart.

- Example Prayer: "Lord, I give You my anxieties, worries, and fears. Help me trust in Your timing and rest in the knowledge that You are in control."

Step 2: Meditate on God's Promises

Find verses that resonate with you and meditate on them throughout the day. Reflecting on God's promises strengthens faith and provides reassurance in moments of doubt.

- Verse Suggestions: Meditate on Psalms 46:10 ("Be still, and know that I am God"), and Psalm 55:22 ("Cast your burden on the Lord, and He shall sustain you").

Step 3: Practice Mindful Patience

Mindfulness can help increase patience by grounding us in the present. Practice breathing deeply and repeating a calming phrase, such as "God is with me," whenever feelings of impatience arise.

Step 4: Seek Fellowship and Encouragement

Engaging with a faith community can provide encouragement and perspective. Surround yourself with those who support your spiritual journey and offer reminders of God's faithfulness.

5. Conclusion: Finding Peace in God's Perfect Timing

Trusting in divine timing and surrendering our worries to God can be transformative, offering relief from the mental strain of depression. As we learn to release control and embrace God's timing, we allow Him to work within us, renewing our strength and restoring our hope. Remember that God's timing is always perfect, even if it does not align with our desires. In surrender, we find not only peace but also a sense of purpose, as we come to understand that each season is part of His plan for our growth.

By practicing patience and trusting in God's care, we open ourselves to His healing power, experiencing the freedom that comes from placing our burdens in His hands. Through divine timing and surrender, we discover a peace that transcends understanding, bringing comfort and hope even in the midst of life's most challenging moments.

Divine Timing—Everything You Need to Know

Understanding Divine Timing: What It Is and Why It Matters

Divine timing is the belief that events in life unfold at the right time according to a higher plan. It encourages us to let go of fears and anxieties, trusting that God or the universe orchestrates events for our highest good. Divine timing does not necessarily mean waiting passively; rather, it involves cultivating patience, faith, and a deep awareness of how each experience can lead to growth and fulfillment.

Divine timing is found throughout the Bible, reminding us of God's precise timing in all things. Ecclesiastes 3:1 says, "To everything there is a season, and a time for every purpose under heaven." This verse highlights the divine rhythm in life, where everything we encounter—be it joy, sorrow, success, or failure—has a unique purpose.

1. What Is Divine Timing?

Divine timing is the concept of allowing events in life to unfold naturally, without force or resistance. It invites us to accept that life is aligned with God's will, even when we may not fully understand it. According to Proverbs 16:9, "The heart of man plans his way, but the Lord establishes his steps." While we make plans, divine timing determines the outcomes, guiding us toward our true path.

Key Insights into Divine Timing:

- Trust and Surrender: Divine timing requires faith in the unseen, knowing that God's plan is unfolding, even when we cannot see the bigger picture.

- Personal Growth: It often involves challenges and lessons that push us to grow and transform in ways we may not choose on our own.

- Increased Awareness: Divine timing encourages us to remain open to signs, synchronicities, and subtle guidance from God.

2. Signs of Divine Timing

Recognizing divine timing often involves noticing signs that you're on the right path. These signs, sometimes called "synchronicities," serve as reminders that a higher power is at work.

- Synchronicities or Meaningful Coincidences: Seeing repetitive numbers, meeting people unexpectedly, or finding messages that resonate deeply with your situation can indicate divine timing.

- Intuition and Gut Feelings: A deep sense or inner knowing guides you to make specific choices, even if they defy logic.

- Obstacles and Challenges as Redirection: Sometimes, delays or barriers appear not to hinder us, but to redirect us toward something better. Romans 8:28 reminds us, "And we know that in all things God works for the good of those who love him, who have been called according to his purpose."

- A Craving for Change or Transition: Feeling restless or yearning for new beginnings may be a sign that God is leading you to a new season in your life.

3. Positive Associations with Divine Timing

Accepting divine timing can positively impact mental health, reduce anxiety, and increase self-awareness. When we let go and trust that God is guiding us, we find greater peace and clarity.

- Sense of Purpose: Believing in divine timing helps us see every event as part of a larger plan, giving us a clearer sense of direction and purpose.

- Self-Awareness: Embracing divine timing deepens self-awareness, as we become more attuned to our thoughts, emotions, and how God is working within us.

- Reduced Anxiety and Stress: Without the need to control every detail, we are free to live in the moment, trusting that God's timing is always perfect.

As stated in Isaiah 55:8-9, "For my thoughts are not your thoughts, neither are your ways my ways, declares the Lord. As the heavens are higher than the earth, so are my ways higher than your ways and my thoughts than your thoughts." This powerful reminder encourages us to relinquish control and rest in God's timing.

4. How to Manifest Divine Timing

While we cannot control divine timing, we can align ourselves to make the most of it. By practicing faith and openness, we can become more receptive to God's guidance.

Step 1: Set Clear Intentions

Identify what you truly desire in life. Be specific about your goals, dreams, and aspirations. According to Psalm 37:4, "Delight yourself in the Lord, and he will give you the desires of your heart." By focusing on what brings you closer to God, you align your intentions with His plan for you.

Step 2: Practice Patience

Divine timing may not align with our expectations, so patience is essential. The Bible emphasizes patience as a virtue in James 1:4: "But let patience have her perfect work, that ye may be perfect and entire, wanting nothing." Trust that every delay serves a purpose in God's design.

Step 3: Trust in God's Plan

Faith in God's wisdom is central to understanding divine timing. Even when outcomes don't immediately favor us, remember that God has a greater plan in mind. Proverbs 3:5-6 reminds us, "Trust in the Lord with all your heart, and lean not on your own understanding. In all your ways acknowledge him, and he will make straight your paths."

Step 4: Take Steps Toward Your Goals

Although divine timing calls for patience, it doesn't mean inaction. We are encouraged to work toward our goals while trusting God to open the right doors. James 2:17 emphasizes that "faith by itself, if it does not have works, is dead." Taking action demonstrates our commitment and helps align our lives with God's divine purpose.

5. Divine Timing in Times of Uncertainty

In times of depression or mental health struggles, trusting in divine timing can offer hope. Believing that God has a plan, even amid hardship, encourages us to surrender our pain to Him, knowing that each challenge has meaning. Psalm 46:10 says, "Be still, and know that I am God." This verse reminds us that in times of uncertainty, we can find peace by placing our trust in God's hands.

Trusting divine timing also reduces the mental strain of "what if" thinking. By focusing on the present moment and surrendering outcomes to God, we can break free from cycles of fear and regret. Embracing divine timing fosters resilience, helping us see trials as temporary seasons that serve our growth and transformation.

Living in Alignment with Divine Timing

Divine timing is a powerful reminder that every moment has purpose, even if we cannot yet perceive it. By trusting in God's wisdom, releasing control, and embracing the present, we align ourselves with a higher rhythm, one that leads us to fulfillment and peace. Remember that God's timing is always perfect, and through patience and faith, we can rest assured that everything unfolds exactly as it should.

As Galatians 6:9 encourages, "Let us not be weary in well-doing, for in due season we shall reap, if we faint not." Divine timing invites us to hold onto hope, trust in God's purpose, and allow Him to guide us along the path He has lovingly prepared.

CHAPTER 08

FACING YOUR FEARS – HOW AVOIDANCE WORSENS DEPRESSION

Fear is a natural response to uncertainty or perceived threats, but when it becomes overwhelming, it can drive us to avoid certain situations, people, or responsibilities. Although avoidance might offer temporary relief, it can often deepen feelings of helplessness and worsen symptoms of depression over time. Psychologists recognize this pattern as a cycle where fear avoidance compounds anxiety, reduces self-confidence, and reinforces the depressive state. Understanding and facing our fears is a powerful step toward healing and regaining control over life.

1. The Role of Fear and Avoidance in Mental Health

Fear is an emotional response that serves an essential purpose: it alerts us to potential dangers and encourages caution. However, when fear grows unchecked, it can lead to avoidance behaviors that limit personal growth and social engagement. Avoidance becomes a coping mechanism, helping people temporarily escape uncomfortable feelings. However, when consistently used, avoidance often leads to a cycle of fear, self-doubt, and depression. Psychologist David Barlow, a leading researcher in anxiety and depression, explains that avoiding a feared task or responsibility can deepen feelings of inadequacy and prolong the fear itself.

According to Cognitive Behavioral Therapy (CBT), one of the most effective therapies for anxiety and depression, avoidance reinforces negative beliefs about oneself. For example, when someone avoids social situations due to fear of judgment, they unintentionally reinforce the belief that they are unworthy or incapable of handling social interactions. This belief, in turn, deepens depression and reduces self-confidence.

2. How Avoidance Worsens Depression

Avoidance has several damaging effects on mental health, including the following:

- Feelings of Helplessness and Hopelessness: Avoidance often leads to a sense of helplessness, as people feel unable to manage their responsibilities. This helplessness can progress into hopelessness, a core feature of depression.

- Isolation and Loneliness: Avoiding social situations to escape judgment or embarrassment can result in isolation and loneliness, further exacerbating depressive symptoms.

- Reinforcing Negative Beliefs: When people avoid tasks or challenges, they affirm their fears and negative beliefs, solidifying feelings of unworthiness or incompetence.

- Increased Anxiety: Ironically, avoiding feared situations can increase anxiety because the fear never gets confronted or managed, resulting in a constant feeling of "waiting" for anxiety to strike.

A study published in the Journal of Anxiety Disorders found that people who habitually avoid difficult situations or emotions are more likely to experience severe depression than those who confront their fears. This research supports the CBT view that avoidance undermines mental resilience and contributes to the cycle of anxiety and depression.

3. Psychological Perspectives on Fear and Avoidance

From a psychological standpoint, avoidance can be described as an unhelpful coping strategy that impairs personal growth. Here are some perspectives from psychologists on how avoidance affects mental health and contributes to depression:

- Learned Helplessness: Psychologist Martin Seligman's concept of "learned helplessness" demonstrates how repeated avoidance leads people to feel incapable of changing their situations. As people avoid challenges, they reinforce the belief that they are powerless, which intensifies depression.

- Fear Conditioning: Fear avoidance can also be explained by fear conditioning, a theory proposed by behaviorist John Watson. According to Watson, when people avoid situations due to fear, they condition themselves to fear those situations even more. This conditioning leads to "catastrophizing," where minor concerns are exaggerated and anticipated as overwhelming.

- Reinforcement Theory: Avoidance is reinforced because it offers immediate relief from anxiety, a concept rooted in the principles of reinforcement. However, this short-term relief only strengthens the avoidance behavior, making it harder to face fears later on. Over time, avoidance leads to diminished self-efficacy—the belief in one's ability to cope effectively—which is strongly linked to depression.

4. Why Facing Your Fears Is Essential for Recovery

Facing fears is a fundamental aspect of overcoming avoidance and moving toward recovery from depression. Psychologists emphasize that gradually confronting fears and challenging avoidance behaviors is crucial for building self-confidence, resilience, and a sense of control.

- Exposure Therapy: Exposure therapy is a technique used to help people confront and overcome their fears gradually. By repeatedly facing a feared situation in a controlled environment, individuals learn that the situation is not as threatening as they believed. Over time, they feel less anxiety, and their confidence grows.

- Breaking the Cycle of Fear: When people face their fears, they interrupt the cycle of avoidance that contributes to depression. Facing fears challenges negative beliefs and fosters a sense of accomplishment, helping individuals feel more capable and resilient.

- Building Self-Efficacy: Self-efficacy, or the belief in one's ability to overcome obstacles, is essential for mental well-being. Facing fears strengthens self-efficacy by showing individuals that they can handle difficult situations, reducing feelings of helplessness.

- Emotional Processing: Facing fears also allows for emotional processing, helping people release pent-up emotions and reduce the mental burden of avoiding distressing thoughts or situations.

5. Practical Steps for Facing Your Fears

Facing fears doesn't mean tackling everything at once. Taking gradual steps, practicing self-compassion, and seeking support are essential to making this journey effective and sustainable.

Step 1: Acknowledge the Fear

Recognize and name your fears. By identifying the specific fear, you can better understand what triggers your avoidance. Ask yourself questions like:

- What am I avoiding, and why?

- How does avoiding this fear make me feel?

Step 2: Take Small Steps

Set small, manageable goals to confront your fear. For instance, if you fear social situations, start by engaging in brief conversations with friends or family. Gradual exposure helps you build confidence and experience small victories along the way.

Step 3: Challenge Negative Thoughts

Examine any negative beliefs that reinforce your avoidance, such as "I'll fail," or "I can't handle this." Replace them with balanced thoughts like "I've handled similar situations before," or "Even if it's challenging, I'll learn from it." This approach, known as cognitive restructuring, helps shift the focus from fear to constructive thinking.

Step 4: Practice Self-Compassion

Avoid being overly self-critical if progress is slow. Self-compassion involves treating yourself with kindness and understanding, which is essential for overcoming fear.

Research in the Journal of Clinical Psychology shows that self-compassion reduces anxiety and helps build resilience.

Step 5: Seek Social Support

Connecting with others who encourage and support you can make facing fears less daunting. Surround yourself with positive influences, join support groups, or speak with friends who understand your situation.

Step 6: Reflect on Progress

As you confront your fears, take time to reflect on your achievements. Even small steps are victories that signal growth. Acknowledge how far you've come, and reinforce the belief that facing fears is possible.

6. Faith and Overcoming Fear

Many spiritual traditions offer comfort in times of fear, reminding us of a divine presence that walks alongside us through struggles. For example, in the Bible, Isaiah 41:10 says, "Fear not, for I am with you; be not dismayed, for I am your God. I will strengthen you, I will help you, I will uphold you with my righteous right hand." Recognizing a higher power can be an anchor that provides peace and courage when facing life's challenges.

Additionally, Psalm 23:4 offers reassurance: "Even though I walk through the valley of the shadow of death, I will fear no evil, for you are with me." Faith can offer the strength to face fears without avoidance, trusting that a higher power is guiding the way.

Embracing Courage in the Journey to Recovery

Avoidance, while seemingly protective, can trap us in a cycle of fear, isolation, and depression. Facing fears is essential for personal growth, mental clarity, and self-compassion. By confronting avoidance step by step, we strengthen our resilience, rebuild self-confidence, and reclaim control over our lives. Trusting that growth lies on the other side of fear can empower us to take the first step toward healing and liberation from depression.

Strategies for Facing Challenges—Steps to Regain Control and Combat Depression

Introduction: The Importance of Facing Challenges

Facing challenges is a fundamental part of personal growth and resilience. While it's natural to want to avoid discomfort, consistently evading our fears and challenges can reinforce feelings of helplessness and deepen depressive symptoms. Developing strategies to confront our fears, build resilience, and regain control over our lives is essential to mental well-being. In this chapter, we will examine practical steps for facing challenges and how these strategies can empower individuals to reduce depressive symptoms and regain a sense of purpose.

We'll incorporate insights from psychology, theology, and practical guidance to offer a comprehensive approach to overcoming life's hurdles.

1. Understanding the Role of Challenges in Personal Growth

From a psychological perspective, challenges are opportunities for growth. When we confront difficult situations or emotions, we strengthen our capacity to handle future adversity, building resilience in the process. Facing challenges involves cognitive, emotional, and behavioral shifts, where we change not only how we think but also how we feel and act in response to our fears.

In the realm of theology, challenges can be viewed as opportunities for spiritual growth and reliance on divine guidance. The Bible teaches that trials are part of the human experience and that we grow stronger in our faith when we trust in God's support during difficult times. James 1:2–4, for instance, tells us, "Consider it pure joy, my brothers and sisters, whenever you face trials of many kinds, because you know that the testing of your faith produces perseverance. Let perseverance finish its work so that you may be mature and complete, not lacking anything." Through this lens, challenges are not merely obstacles but are tools for refining our character.

2. Key Psychological Theories on Facing Fears and Overcoming Challenges

Cognitive-Behavioral Therapy (CBT): Rewiring Thought Patterns

One of the most effective approaches to facing fears and challenges is rooted in Cognitive-Behavioral Therapy (CBT). This therapy emphasizes identifying and challenging negative thought patterns and gradually changing behaviors that maintain anxiety or depression.

CBT introduces the concept of "exposure," where individuals gradually confront feared situations, allowing them to realize that their fears may be less daunting than imagined. This exposure technique, combined with cognitive restructuring (challenging and reframing negative thoughts), is a powerful way to break free from the cycle of avoidance that often exacerbates depression.

Resilience Theory: Building Emotional Endurance

Resilience Theory posits that individuals can build "psychological resilience" by overcoming adversity, which in turn strengthens their ability to handle future difficulties. This theory highlights the role of adaptive coping mechanisms, such as problem-solving, seeking social support, and using positive self-talk, to help individuals manage challenges effectively. By practicing resilience-building techniques, people not only survive hardships but thrive, experiencing greater emotional stability and mental well-being.

The Role of Meaning-Making: Viktor Frankl's Logotherapy

Logotherapy, developed by psychiatrist Viktor Frankl, emphasizes finding meaning in life's experiences, especially during difficult times. According to Frankl, individuals who attach meaning to their struggles are better able to endure them and emerge with renewed purpose. This sense of meaning is particularly significant in overcoming depressive symptoms, as it shifts one's focus from hopelessness to hope and purpose.

3. Practical Steps to Face Challenges and Regain Control

Step 1: Set Small, Achievable Goals

When facing a challenge, it can be overwhelming to tackle it all at once. Instead, break down the task or problem into smaller, manageable steps. Set realistic goals that are achievable within a short timeframe. For example, if social anxiety is an issue, the first goal might be simply to greet someone in passing. Each small accomplishment provides a sense of achievement, reinforcing self-confidence and building momentum.

Step 2: Develop Positive Self-Talk and Reframe Negative Thoughts

Challenge negative thoughts that emerge when facing a difficult situation. Replace thoughts like "I can't handle this" with "I can take small steps to manage this situation." Positive self-talk is essential to rewiring our beliefs about ourselves and our abilities, transforming obstacles into opportunities for growth.

Biblically, Philippians 4:13 reminds us, "I can do all things through Christ who strengthens me." This verse serves as a powerful affirmation, providing comfort and motivation when confronting challenges.

Step 3: Practice Mindfulness and Emotional Awareness

Mindfulness, the practice of staying present in the moment, allows individuals to observe their thoughts and emotions without judgment. When we confront challenges, we may feel a rush of anxiety or fear. Practicing mindfulness can help manage these emotions and prevent them from overwhelming us. Regular mindfulness exercises, such as deep breathing or meditation, promote clarity and calm, making it easier to approach challenges rationally.

Step 4: Use the "What-If" Technique for Facing Fears

The "What-If" technique involves thinking through the potential outcomes of facing a fear or challenge. Ask yourself, "What if this fear actually happens? What could I do?" Often, when we analyze the potential outcomes rationally, they seem less intimidating. This technique helps break the catastrophic thinking pattern that often paralyzes us in the face of fear.

Step 5: Lean on Spiritual Beliefs for Strength and Guidance

Turning to faith during challenging times can offer comfort, perspective, and guidance. By trusting in divine timing and seeking spiritual strength, individuals can feel less alone and more equipped to face their fears. Proverbs 3:5–6 advises, "Trust in the Lord with all your heart and lean not on your own understanding; in all your ways submit to him, and he will make your paths straight." Believing that a higher power has a plan for us helps cultivate patience and resilience.

Step 6: Build a Support System

Social support is invaluable when confronting challenges. Surrounding oneself with friends, family, or support groups provides encouragement, accountability, and a sense of connection. Share your fears or struggles with others who understand and can offer guidance. Not only does this make challenges feel less daunting, but it also strengthens emotional bonds, which is essential for mental well-being.

4. Theological Perspective: Trusting God's Plan and Finding Purpose in Challenges

In many religious teachings, challenges are seen as part of a divine plan, opportunities for growth, and acts of faith. Trusting in divine timing and the wisdom of a higher power can bring peace during difficult times, reducing stress and anxiety.

For instance, in Romans 8:28, we are told, "And we know that in all things God works for the good of those who love him, who have been called according to his purpose." This verse reminds believers that even challenging experiences can serve a greater purpose in their lives. Accepting this perspective can relieve the pressure to control every outcome and bring comfort in trusting that one's struggles have meaning.

5. Overcoming Common Barriers to Facing Challenges

Overthinking and Analysis Paralysis

One major obstacle to facing challenges is overthinking, where individuals become so focused on potential outcomes that they become immobilized. To overcome this, use the "Just Start" technique: take a small action to begin, without overanalyzing. By taking small steps, you gain momentum and reduce the paralyzing effects of overthinking.

Fear of Failure

Fear of failure often prevents people from confronting challenges. However, failure can be an opportunity to learn and grow. Embrace failure as a natural part of the process, focusing on the lessons learned rather than the setback itself.

Perfectionism

Perfectionism can create unrealistic standards, making challenges seem insurmountable. Challenge this mindset by adopting a "progress over perfection" attitude, where effort and improvement are valued over flawless results.

The Power of Facing Challenges

Facing challenges is a journey of self-discovery, resilience, and growth. From a psychological perspective, confronting fears directly enables us to break the cycle of avoidance, leading to greater self-confidence and reduced depressive symptoms. From a theological standpoint, challenges are seen as part of God's plan, giving purpose to our struggles and offering opportunities to strengthen our faith.

By setting small, achievable goals, cultivating positive self-talk, practicing mindfulness, and leaning on spiritual beliefs, we can regain control over our lives and emerge stronger. As the Psalmist wrote in Psalm 46:1, "God is our refuge and strength, an ever-present help in trouble." Through faith, psychological strategies, and resilience-building practices, individuals can face challenges with courage and hope, turning obstacles into stepping stones on the path to mental well-being.

Courage in Faith—Drawing Strength from Biblical Teachings to Overcome Depression

Introduction: The Need for Spiritual Courage in Overcoming Life's Challenges

In times of hardship, fear, or uncertainty, the Bible offers a wealth of wisdom, encouraging believers to draw courage from faith. Theological and spiritual teachings inspire individuals to face adversity with strength, resilience, and hope rooted in God's promises. For those struggling with depression, understanding and embracing these teachings can provide a sense of peace, comfort, and purpose that transcends ordinary coping mechanisms.

Depression often creates feelings of helplessness, unworthiness, and hopelessness. Reflecting on biblical stories and spiritual principles can remind believers that they are not alone—that God's presence is with them, guiding them through every challenge. In this chapter, we will explore biblical stories, verses, and the importance of courage in faith, examining how a close relationship with God empowers individuals to confront life's trials with confidence and trust.

1. Biblical Teachings on Courage and Strength

The Bible repeatedly reminds us that God is our ultimate source of strength and courage, a rock we can rely on even in our darkest moments. Scripture teaches that faith gives us the ability to confront our fears, not because we are strong in ourselves, but because God's strength is within us.

In Deuteronomy 31:6, Moses assures the Israelites, "Be strong and courageous. Do not be afraid or terrified because of them, for the Lord your God goes with you; he will never leave you nor forsake you." This verse conveys God's unwavering presence and support, reassuring us that our courage is grounded in His unchanging faithfulness. Reflecting on this truth during difficult times reminds us that we are not alone in our struggles and that God's power is greater than any fear or challenge we face.

2. Why Spiritual Courage is Essential in Fighting Depression

Depression can cloud one's perception, creating a sense of isolation and worthlessness. Faith-based courage, however, serves as a powerful antidote. When we draw on God's promises, we become more resilient, realizing that our identity and worth are rooted in Him and not in our circumstances. This courage grounded in faith enables us to face our inner fears and the lies that depression often whispers—fears of failure, rejection, or insignificance—by anchoring our trust in God's truth and love.

Psalm 34:17–18 assures believers that "The righteous cry out, and the Lord hears them; he delivers them from all their troubles. The Lord is close to the brokenhearted and saves those who are crushed in spirit." Here, the Psalmist emphasizes that God is close to those who are suffering, reminding us that our pain does not go unnoticed by Him. This proximity of God to the brokenhearted offers a profound source of courage, giving believers the strength to endure, knowing that God's healing presence is ever near.

3. Biblical Stories of Courage as Examples for Believers

The Bible is rich with stories of individuals who, despite facing immense challenges, demonstrated courage through faith. By examining these stories, believers can find role models who trusted God amidst overwhelming fear, despair, and uncertainty.

3.1 David and Goliath (1 Samuel 17)

One of the most renowned stories of courage in the Bible is David's battle against Goliath. David, a young shepherd, was not a trained soldier, yet he had a deep faith in

God. When he faced Goliath, he did not rely on physical strength or weapons but on his belief in God's power to deliver him. David boldly declared, "The Lord who rescued me from the paw of the lion and the paw of the bear will rescue me from the hand of this Philistine" (1 Samuel 17:37).

David's courage in facing Goliath reflects the power of trusting in God rather than one's abilities. For believers facing the "giants" of depression, this story serves as a reminder that courage comes from recognizing God's power and presence. Just as David overcame the odds through faith, so too can believers find strength to confront the giants of fear, doubt, and despair.

3.2 Elijah and the Still Small Voice (1 Kings 19)

The prophet Elijah faced extreme fear and isolation when Queen Jezebel threatened his life. He fled into the wilderness, feeling defeated and asking God to take his life, a moment that echoes the despair many experience in depression. However, God responded not by rebuking Elijah's fear, but by providing comfort and strength. God appeared to Elijah, not in a grand display, but in a "gentle whisper," reminding him of His presence and love (1 Kings 19:12–13).

Elijah's story illustrates that God meets us even in our moments of deepest despair. When depression makes us feel isolated and weak, we can find courage in knowing that God's presence is quiet but constant. He whispers to us in our darkness, providing the peace and guidance needed to persevere.

3.3 Paul's Perseverance Amid Hardship (2 Corinthians 12:7–10)

The Apostle Paul endured numerous hardships, including persecution, imprisonment, and personal struggles. In 2 Corinthians, Paul describes a "thorn in the flesh" that he prayed for God to remove, but God's response was, "My grace is sufficient for you, for my power is made perfect in weakness" (2 Corinthians 12:9). Paul's faith enabled him to embrace his weaknesses as a means for God's strength to be displayed in his life.

Paul's story encourages believers to see their struggles as opportunities for God's grace to shine. Depression can often feel like an unmovable "thorn," but just as Paul found courage in his weakness, so too can believers draw strength from knowing that God's grace is sufficient in all circumstances.

4. Key Bible Verses on Courage and Faith

- Isaiah 41:10: "So do not fear, for I am with you; do not be dismayed, for I am your God. I will strengthen you and help you; I will uphold you with my righteous right hand."

This verse reassures believers that God's presence brings strength and support, diminishing fear.

- Joshua 1:9: "Have I not commanded you? Be strong and courageous. Do not be afraid; do not be discouraged, for the Lord your God will be with you wherever you go." This command to be courageous reminds believers that courage is not optional—it is essential for faith.

- Psalm 23:4: "Even though I walk through the darkest valley, I will fear no evil, for you are with me; your rod and your staff, they comfort me." This well-loved verse conveys the peace that comes from knowing God's protective presence during life's trials.

5. Practical Ways to Cultivate Courage Through Faith

Reflect on God's Promises Daily

Meditating on verses that highlight God's strength, presence, and promises can reinforce one's faith and courage. Reading and reflecting on these truths daily builds mental and spiritual resilience, providing the courage to face each day's challenges.

Prayer and Surrender

Turning to God in prayer, especially during moments of fear or despair, strengthens our relationship with Him. Surrendering our worries and burdens to God reminds us that we don't have to carry our burdens alone. Matthew 11:28 reminds us, "Come to me, all you who are weary and burdened, and I will give you rest." This act of surrender provides relief from the weight of depression.

Join a Faith Community

Engaging in fellowship with other believers who support and encourage one another reinforces courage. Faith communities often provide encouragement, accountability, and wisdom. As Ecclesiastes 4:9–10 states, "Two are better than one, because they have a good return for their labor: If either of them falls down, one can help the other up." In times of difficulty, fellow believers offer reminders of God's promises and help us remain steadfast.

Serve Others in Love

Shifting focus from personal struggles to helping others can renew courage and purpose. Acts of service are spiritually uplifting, as serving others reflects God's love. By blessing others, believers also feel empowered and fulfilled, which can alleviate feelings of despair.

Conclusion: Embracing Courage in Faith to Combat Depression

Courage grounded in faith is not the absence of fear, but the decision to trust God in the midst of it. Biblical and spiritual teachings on courage remind believers that they are not alone in their struggles—God is always present, guiding and strengthening them. Through stories like David's confrontation with Goliath, Elijah's encounter with God in the wilderness, and Paul's perseverance, we learn that courage is possible even in the darkest times.

Trusting in God's promises, relying on His strength, and reflecting on His presence empower us to face life's challenges with resilience. Depression may make the path seem difficult, but courage rooted in faith can lead to healing, restoration, and a life filled with hope.

CHAPTER 09

SUNLIGHT AND MENTAL HEALTH-UNDERSTANDING THE POSITIVE IMPACT OF SUNLIGHT ON MOOD AND WELL-BEING

Introduction: The Healing Power of Sunlight

Throughout history, sunlight has been celebrated for its ability to promote physical and emotional well-being. Often referred to as a natural "mood booster," sunlight plays a crucial role in our mental health by stimulating biological processes that positively affect our minds and bodies. The exposure to natural light, particularly in the morning, has been shown to regulate mood, improve sleep quality, and support overall mental health.

This chapter delves into the scientific and psychological effects of sunlight on mental health, focusing on how sunlight influences the brain's production of mood-regulating chemicals like serotonin. By understanding the connection between sunlight and mood, individuals can incorporate regular exposure to natural light as part of a holistic approach to reducing symptoms of depression, anxiety, and other mood-related conditions.

1. The Science Behind Sunlight and Mood

The relationship between sunlight and mood is largely linked to the brain's production of serotonin, a neurotransmitter that contributes to feelings of happiness and well-being. When our skin absorbs sunlight, it triggers a complex series of reactions that ultimately result in an increase in serotonin levels.

1.1 Serotonin: The "Feel-Good" Chemical

Serotonin is a neurotransmitter that influences mood, social behavior, appetite, sleep, memory, and sexual desire. Higher levels of serotonin are associated with better mood, while lower levels are linked to depression and anxiety. Sunlight exposure increases serotonin production in the brain, which in turn elevates mood and helps counter feelings of sadness or lethargy.

Research shows that serotonin levels are naturally lower during the darker months of the year and higher when days are longer, indicating that exposure to sunlight directly impacts serotonin levels. This connection explains why people often feel more energized and positive during spring and summer, and why reduced sunlight exposure in winter can lead to a condition known as Seasonal Affective Disorder (SAD).

1.2 The Role of Vitamin D

Sunlight also plays a vital role in the synthesis of Vitamin D, which supports immune health, bone density, and mental well-being. When ultraviolet B (UVB) rays from the sun hit the skin, they trigger the production of Vitamin D, an essential nutrient for many bodily functions, including brain health.

Low levels of Vitamin D have been linked to depression and cognitive impairment. Regular exposure to sunlight, therefore, serves as a natural source of Vitamin D, promoting better mental health by reducing the likelihood of Vitamin D deficiency and its associated symptoms.

2. Psychological Benefits of Sunlight Exposure

Sunlight affects more than just our physical health; it also has profound psychological benefits. From improving mood to reducing anxiety, exposure to natural light positively influences mental health in several ways.

2.1 Improved Mood and Reduced Anxiety

Research indicates that sunlight exposure has an antidepressant effect due to its influence on serotonin production. Even short periods spent outdoors can help alleviate symptoms of mild to moderate depression. The release of serotonin helps counteract stress hormones and reduce anxiety, providing a sense of calm and contentment.

Additionally, spending time in sunlight can foster a sense of connection to the natural world, which has been shown to enhance mood and reduce feelings of loneliness. For those who may feel isolated or disconnected, sunlight and nature exposure can provide an uplifting experience, promoting mental clarity and relaxation.

2.2 Enhanced Sleep Quality and Regulation of Circadian Rhythms

Sunlight exposure, particularly in the morning, helps regulate our body's internal clock or circadian rhythm. This rhythm dictates our sleep-wake cycle, affecting when we feel alert and when we feel tired. Proper exposure to natural light during the day, especially early in the morning, helps regulate this rhythm, leading to better quality sleep.

When circadian rhythms are properly aligned, individuals experience improved mental clarity, reduced fatigue, and lower levels of stress. Conversely, lack of sunlight exposure can disrupt sleep patterns, resulting in poor sleep quality, irritability, and mental exhaustion—all of which can contribute to a decline in mental health.

2.3 Reduced Symptoms of Seasonal Affective Disorder (SAD)

Seasonal Affective Disorder (SAD) is a type of depression that occurs in response to seasonal changes, often during the darker winter months. SAD is thought to be triggered by a reduction in sunlight exposure, which decreases serotonin production. For individuals with SAD, sunlight exposure or light therapy (using a lightbox that mimics natural sunlight) has proven effective in alleviating symptoms.

Light therapy mimics the effect of natural sunlight and can help reset the body's internal clock, reduce depressive symptoms, and improve mood. For individuals with SAD, regular sunlight exposure or light therapy is a crucial component of mental health management, especially in regions with limited sunlight during winter.

3. Practical Ways to Incorporate Sunlight for Mental Health Benefits

Given the profound impact of sunlight on mental well-being, incorporating regular exposure to natural light can be an effective way to boost mood, reduce anxiety, and support overall mental health. Here are practical tips for maximizing the benefits of sunlight exposure.

3.1 Spend Time Outdoors Daily

Even just 15–30 minutes of sunlight exposure each day can significantly improve mood and increase Vitamin D levels. Activities such as walking, gardening, or sitting outside during daylight hours provide a natural, accessible way to increase sunlight exposure.

3.2 Seek Morning Sunlight

Exposing yourself to natural light in the morning is especially beneficial for regulating circadian rhythms. Morning sunlight exposure helps "set" your internal clock, leading to improved energy levels and better sleep quality at night. Try to spend time outdoors or near a window in the morning whenever possible.

3.3 Use Light Therapy if Necessary

For individuals living in regions with limited sunlight or for those with Seasonal Affective Disorder, light therapy can be a helpful alternative to natural sunlight. Light therapy devices are designed to emit light that mimics sunlight and can be used during the darker months to maintain serotonin levels and stabilize mood.

4. Biblical and Theological Insights on Sunlight and Creation

The Bible often highlights the importance of sunlight as part of God's creation. In Genesis 1:3, God says, "Let there be light," underscoring light as a fundamental and life-giving aspect of creation. Light is not only essential for physical life but also symbolizes spiritual clarity, joy, and divine presence throughout scripture.

In Ecclesiastes 11:7, we read, "Light is sweet, and it pleases the eyes to see the sun." This verse captures the beauty and comfort of sunlight, reflecting its importance for human well-being. Sunlight, in a theological sense, represents God's provision for both physical and spiritual health.

Psalm 118:24 and the Gift of Each Day

Psalm 118:24 reminds us, "This is the day the Lord has made; let us rejoice and be glad in it." This verse encourages gratitude for each day and the blessings it brings, including sunlight. Recognizing sunlight as part of God's provision inspires us to enjoy the natural world and prioritize health practices, such as spending time outdoors, as a form of gratitude and care for the life God has given us.

5. Conclusion: Embracing Sunlight as Part of a Holistic Mental Health Approach

Sunlight offers powerful and natural benefits for mental health, positively influencing mood, regulating sleep patterns, and supporting a healthy circadian rhythm. As we have seen, sunlight stimulates the production of serotonin and Vitamin D, both crucial for maintaining emotional well-being. Whether facing mild depression, anxiety, or the seasonal effects of limited sunlight, incorporating regular exposure to natural light can improve one's mental health and foster a renewed sense of well-being.

By understanding the science behind sunlight and mood, along with biblical teachings that emphasize light as a divine gift, we can appreciate the role of sunlight in a holistic approach to mental health. Embracing the healing power of sunlight is a simple, effective, and accessible way to nurture both body and soul, reminding us that in the light of God's creation, there is hope, joy, and peace for each new day.

In the mid-1800s, the world was abuzz with rumors of untold riches lying beneath the surface of the earth. The discovery of gold in a remote, uncharted territory set the stage for a historic event – the Gold Rush. Chapter One introduces readers to the protagonists, John and Emily, who are drawn to the promise of fortune and adventure.

Getting Enough Sunlight — Practical Ways to Increase Sunlight Exposure, Even in Winter Months

Introduction: The Importance of Sunlight for Mental and Physical Well-being

Sunlight plays a pivotal role in regulating our moods, sleep cycles, and overall health. Exposure to natural light is directly linked to the brain's production of serotonin, a hormone that promotes feelings of well-being and happiness.

It also influences melatonin levels, a hormone essential for regulating sleep. Without adequate sunlight, especially during winter months or in restrictive environments like prisons, individuals may experience mental health challenges, including mood instability, depression, and even cognitive impairment. This chapter explores practical ways to increase sunlight exposure, especially in low-light conditions, and delves into the impact of limited sunlight on inmates in maximum-security facilities.

1. The Challenges of Getting Sunlight During Winter Months

The colder months often bring shorter days and reduced sunlight, making it harder for people to spend time outdoors. This can lead to Seasonal Affective Disorder (SAD) and other mood-related issues. SAD, in particular, is a type of depression triggered by changes in seasons, primarily due to the reduction in natural light exposure. For those living in regions with extreme winters or for people who have restricted outdoor access, finding ways to incorporate sunlight into their routine can be challenging but vital.

2. Practical Ways to Increase Sunlight Exposure During Winter

Even with limited sunlight in winter, there are effective ways to maximize light exposure. By making adjustments to daily routines, adding artificial light sources, and incorporating mindful practices, individuals can ensure they receive the mental and physical benefits of light exposure.

2.1 Spend Time Outdoors During Peak Sun Hours

When sunlight is limited, it's crucial to make the most of the hours when it's available. In winter, sunlight tends to be strongest between 10 a.m. and 3 p.m. Spending even a few minutes outdoors during this time can help the body absorb beneficial natural light.

Tip: Go for a walk during lunch breaks or sit by a window if going outside isn't possible. The goal is to absorb sunlight whenever it's at its peak, even for a short period.

2.2 Maximize Indoor Sunlight Exposure

Positioning oneself near windows is another way to increase natural light exposure indoors. Working, reading, or relaxing in sunny rooms can help individuals benefit from daylight without needing to go outside in cold temperatures.

Tip: If possible, set up workspaces, eating areas, or leisure spots near windows with maximum sunlight exposure. Pulling back curtains or blinds during the day can also increase light flow into rooms.

2.3 Use Light Therapy or a Light Box

Light therapy is a common and effective solution for combating the mental health effects of limited sunlight. Light boxes, designed to mimic natural sunlight, emit light at an intensity of around 10,000 lux, which is enough to stimulate serotonin production and improve mood.

Tip: Place a light box in a convenient spot and use it for 20-30 minutes each morning. Light therapy works best when it becomes part of a daily routine, ideally in the morning, to align with natural circadian rhythms.

2.4 Try Dawn Simulation Devices

Dawn simulators gradually increase the brightness of a room, mimicking a natural sunrise. They're especially helpful in dark winter months when waking up to darkness can disrupt natural body rhythms. Dawn simulators can help improve mood and energy levels, easing the transition from sleep to wakefulness.

Tip: Set a dawn simulator to begin increasing light intensity 30-45 minutes before waking. This technique can mimic the effect of waking up to natural sunlight, providing an energizing start to the day.

2.5 Incorporate Physical Activity Outdoors

If possible, combining physical activity with sunlight exposure can maximize benefits. Exercise boosts endorphin levels, helping to elevate mood, and when paired with sunlight, it becomes a powerful antidote to winter blues.

Tip: Bundle up and take a brisk walk outdoors during the day. Even brief outdoor activities can provide an effective dose of sunlight and improve mood.

3. The Impact of Limited Sunlight on Inmates in Maximum-Security Prisons

Incarcerated individuals, particularly those in maximum-security facilities, often have restricted access to sunlight. Prolonged confinement indoors can lead to Vitamin D deficiencies, disrupted circadian rhythms, and significant mental health challenges. For inmates who rarely see the sun, the lack of natural light contributes to a range of physical and psychological issues, including:

- Vitamin D Deficiency: Without adequate sunlight exposure, the body struggles to produce sufficient Vitamin D, which is essential for immune function and mental health.

- Mood Instability: The absence of sunlight reduces serotonin levels, which can worsen depression, anxiety, and feelings of despair among inmates.

- Disrupted Sleep Cycles: A lack of natural light disrupts melatonin production, leading to poor sleep quality and difficulty regulating sleep-wake cycles.

- Increased Incidence of Depression and Anxiety: Restricted sunlight exposure in prison settings is strongly associated with increased levels of depression, anxiety, irritability, and aggression.

For individuals in maximum-security facilities, sunlight deprivation can create a feedback loop that exacerbates mental health issues, making confinement significantly more challenging.

4. Solutions to Address the Impact of Sunlight Deprivation in Prisons

To mitigate the harmful effects of sunlight deprivation, correctional facilities can implement strategies to provide inmates with access to natural or artificial light sources. While logistical and security challenges exist, solutions can make a meaningful difference in the mental health of incarcerated individuals.

4.1 Increase Access to Outdoor Spaces

Providing inmates with structured outdoor time, even if brief, can increase sunlight exposure and improve mental health. Access to outdoor spaces where sunlight is available for a designated period helps inmates maintain essential sunlight exposure.

Recommendation: Facilities should aim to create secure outdoor areas or exercise yards where inmates can safely access sunlight.

4.2 Use Light Therapy in Confinement Areas

For inmates with restricted outdoor access, light therapy boxes can simulate the effect of sunlight. These light boxes can be installed in certain areas to ensure that inmates receive enough exposure to improve mood, sleep patterns, and overall well-being.

Recommendation: Light therapy can be incorporated in cells or communal areas where inmates spend most of their time. Scheduled light exposure sessions can make a noticeable difference in mental health outcomes.

4.3 Implement Windows in Designated Areas

Where possible, adding windows or skylights in common areas can help increase exposure to natural light. Designing environments that allow some sunlight to filter through gives inmates access to the mental health benefits associated with natural light.

Recommendation: Retrofit areas to include skylights or windows, particularly in dining areas, recreation rooms, or visitation spaces, to allow more natural light flow.

5. Conclusion: Embracing Sunlight for Mental Health Benefits in All Settings

Whether we're dealing with winter months, restricted access to sunlight, or challenging environments like maximum-security prisons, finding ways to increase exposure to natural or simulated sunlight is vital for mental health. The psychological and physical benefits of sunlight—improved mood, better sleep, enhanced immunity, and reduced risk of depression—are essential for everyone, and understanding these benefits is the first step toward a healthier lifestyle.

This chapter has highlighted strategies for increasing sunlight exposure, such as spending time outdoors during peak sun hours, maximizing indoor light, and using light therapy. For those in extreme environments, such as inmates with limited outdoor access, implementing solutions to bring light into confined spaces can be transformative for mental health and well-being.

Through a combination of these practices, individuals can incorporate the life-giving benefits of sunlight into their daily routines, regardless of external circumstances, helping them foster resilience, well-being, and a healthier outlook on life.

Religious Symbolism of Light and Hope

Introduction: The Significance of Light in Faith and Spirituality

Throughout history, light has served as a powerful symbol in religious texts and traditions, representing hope, divine presence, guidance, and spiritual awakening. Across various faiths, light is seen as a metaphor for the presence of God, the triumph of goodness over evil, and the promise of salvation. In Christian theology, light symbolizes the power of Christ, the Word of God, and the indwelling of the Holy Spirit. This chapter delves into the theological perspectives of light as a symbol of hope, examines its biblical foundations, and explores how understanding the spiritual symbolism of light can bring comfort, clarity, and encouragement.

1. Light as a Symbol of God's Presence

In the Bible, light is frequently associated with God Himself, signifying His holy and powerful presence. In the book of Genesis, we see the first act of creation where God brings light into existence, separating it from darkness, symbolizing the order, life, and divine presence He brings to creation.

- Genesis 1:3: "And God said, 'Let there be light,' and there was light." This act of creation not only introduces physical light into the world but also represents God's order and life. The first words spoken by God reveal the inherent goodness of light as it dispels darkness.

Theological scholars view light as a means of encountering God's holiness and purity. The presence of God is described as radiant, beyond human comprehension, and something that fills the faithful with awe and reverence. This notion is echoed in the visions of prophets who describe God's presence as a brilliant, overpowering light.

- Exodus 34:29-30: When Moses comes down from Mount Sinai after speaking with God, his face shines with light. This light signifies God's glory and reflects the transformative power of being in God's presence.

The Strong's Concordance points to the Hebrew word for light, "or," as a term that embodies brilliance, illumination, and the divine essence. Light in this sense is not merely physical but also deeply spiritual and metaphysical, a representation of God's sustaining power and love for His creation.

2. Jesus Christ as the Light of the World

In the New Testament, Jesus is described as the embodiment of light. He is the guiding force, the source of truth, and the way to eternal life. Jesus as the "Light of the World" symbolizes hope, salvation, and deliverance from spiritual darkness.

- John 8:12: "When Jesus spoke again to the people, he said, 'I am the light of the world. Whoever follows me will never walk in darkness, but will have the light of life.'"

Through this declaration, Jesus positions Himself as the divine light that leads believers out of the darkness of sin and ignorance. This symbolism of Jesus as light resonates with His role as the Redeemer who brings clarity, direction, and eternal hope.

- Psalm 27:1: "The Lord is my light and my salvation—whom shall I fear? The Lord is the stronghold of my life—of whom shall I be afraid?" Here, the psalmist associates God with light, illustrating that God's guidance and protection are akin to the illuminating force that dispels fear and doubt.

Jesus' identification with light not only provides guidance but also ensures believers that they are walking in the truth. Theological interpretations emphasize that following Christ as the light means embracing His teachings, finding strength in His promises, and gaining the courage to face life's challenges with faith.

3. Light as a Guide in Times of Uncertainty

Light, in a theological sense, is often portrayed as a guide through life's darkest and most uncertain moments. As believers journey through life, they encounter periods of doubt, fear, and confusion. Scriptures frequently use light to illustrate God's guidance and the assurance that He is with us even in the most challenging times.

- Psalm 119:105: "Your word is a lamp for my feet, a light on my path." This verse conveys the idea that God's Word is an unwavering source of guidance, providing clarity in times of confusion and darkness.

Believers find solace in the knowledge that God's light will always direct their steps, illuminating their path so they can make wise decisions. When life's difficulties feel overwhelming, many turn to this promise as a reminder that God is actively guiding and protecting them.

Theological scholars also emphasize that the "light on the path" refers not only to specific guidance for immediate challenges but also to a more profound, lifelong sense of direction and purpose. In moments of uncertainty, holding on to the belief in God's guiding light can bring comfort, reduce anxiety, and provide hope.

4. Light as the Victory Over Darkness

In Scripture, light is often juxtaposed with darkness to symbolize the triumph of good over evil, life over death, and hope over despair. Light conquers darkness just as the message of Christ conquers sin and death, illustrating hope's victory over hopelessness.

- John 1:5: "The light shines in the darkness, and the darkness has not overcome it." This passage speaks of the resilience of divine light—it cannot be extinguished by the powers of darkness, making it a powerful metaphor for hope and resilience.

Believers see light as a force that dispels evil and sin, affirming that no matter how challenging circumstances may be, God's light will ultimately prevail. It reflects the Christian assurance that through faith, people can overcome despair, temptation, and suffering, drawing on the strength found in God's presence.

The Strong's Concordance emphasizes the Greek word phos (G5457) for light, used in John 1:5 to mean not only physical light but also "that which brings forth understanding and spiritual insight." This distinction underscores the depth of light as a spiritual force, one that represents knowledge, truth, and the life-giving power of God.

5. Light as Eternal Hope and Salvation

The Bible frequently describes salvation in terms of light, portraying heaven as a place of everlasting light where there is no darkness, pain, or suffering. This eternal light represents the fulfillment of God's promise and the ultimate hope for believers.

- Revelation 21:23-24: "The city does not need the sun or the moon to shine on it, for the glory of God gives it light, and the Lamb is its lamp." The eternal light of heaven signifies a world where God's presence is unbroken and His love is eternal.

This vision of eternal light serves as a powerful image of hope for Christians, reminding them that God's promise of salvation is constant, unchanging, and ultimately triumphant over all darkness. Light, in this sense, is the hope of heaven and the peace that awaits believers.

6. Practical Application: Living as Reflections of Divine Light

The call to be "lights in the world" is not only a theological concept but a practical challenge. Believers are encouraged to embody the virtues of love, kindness, and truth, reflecting God's light through their actions and words.

- Matthew 5:14-16: "You are the light of the world. A town built on a hill cannot be hidden. ... let your light shine before others, that they may see your good deeds and glorify your Father in heaven."

The theological call to be lights in the world emphasizes that believers' actions should reflect God's love and bring hope to others. Acting as lights requires a commitment to faith, integrity, and compassion, serving as examples for others and encouraging hope in times of despair.

Conclusion: Embracing the Symbolism of Light for Hope and Healing

Understanding the religious symbolism of light offers profound comfort and inspiration. In the darkest moments, the reminder that God's light is ever-present helps believers find resilience, hope, and clarity. Through the Scriptures, light emerges as a representation of God's guidance, Christ's salvation, and the Holy Spirit's constant presence. In recognizing the theological power of light, individuals can find strength, focus on their spiritual journeys, and embrace the hope that, with God, no darkness can ultimately prevail.

By reflecting on the symbolism of light and striving to embody its virtues, believers not only experience a deeper connection to their faith but also bring comfort, clarity, and encouragement to those around them.

CHAPTER 10

COGNITIVE BEHAVIORAL THERAPY (CBT)

Introduction: The Power of CBT in Mental Health Treatment

Cognitive Behavioral Therapy (CBT) is one of the most widely used and effective forms of psychological treatment for a range of mental health disorders, including depression. As a therapeutic approach, CBT focuses on identifying and changing negative thought patterns and behaviors that contribute to emotional distress. Unlike some forms of therapy that delve into a person's past to uncover the origins of emotional issues, CBT is future-focused, aiming to equip individuals with practical strategies to address their current challenges. This chapter explains the foundations of CBT, explores how it functions, and discusses its proven effectiveness in treating depression.

1. What is Cognitive Behavioral Therapy (CBT)?

Cognitive Behavioral Therapy is a form of psychotherapy based on the concept that thoughts, feelings, and behaviors are interconnected. It operates under the premise that by altering one's thought patterns (cognitions) and actions (behaviors), one can improve mood and mental well-being.

CBT was developed by psychiatrist Dr. Aaron T. Beck in the 1960s and has since evolved into a structured, time-limited, and goal-oriented approach to therapy. CBT encourages individuals to examine and challenge the validity of their thoughts and beliefs, particularly those that are irrational or overly negative, with the ultimate aim of promoting healthier, more adaptive thinking and behavior patterns.

2. Core Principles of CBT

CBT is grounded in several core principles that distinguish it from other therapeutic approaches:

- Cognitive Restructuring: Central to CBT is the idea that negative thoughts and beliefs can shape one's emotions and behaviors. Cognitive restructuring involves identifying these thoughts and beliefs, examining their accuracy, and replacing them with more realistic, positive perspectives.

- Behavioral Activation: This aspect of CBT addresses the relationship between actions and emotions. In behavioral activation, individuals are encouraged to engage in activities they once enjoyed or that align with their values, even if they initially lack motivation. Over time, these positive activities can help break the cycle of avoidance and low mood associated with depression.

- Problem-Solving Skills: CBT emphasizes teaching effective problem-solving skills. Patients learn how to break down large problems into manageable steps, improving their ability to tackle challenges and reduce feelings of overwhelm.

- Thought Monitoring and Awareness: CBT trains individuals to monitor their thoughts and become more aware of how these thoughts influence their feelings and actions. This awareness is crucial for recognizing patterns of negative thinking that contribute to depression.

3. The CBT Model: The Cognitive Triangle

A central concept in CBT is the Cognitive Triangle — the interaction between thoughts, emotions, and behaviors. This triangle illustrates that changes in any one of these areas can impact the others. For example:

- Thoughts: A person's internal dialogue or beliefs about a situation. In depression, these thoughts are often overly negative or self-critical (e.g., "I'm worthless" or "Things will never get better").

- Emotions: The feelings that arise in response to one's thoughts. In depression, common emotions include sadness, hopelessness, and apathy.

- Behaviors: Actions taken in response to thoughts and emotions. In depression, these behaviors may include withdrawal from social activities, decreased interest in hobbies, or increased isolation.

In CBT, therapists work with patients to modify this cycle by identifying negative or irrational thoughts, challenging their validity, and replacing them with healthier alternatives. As thoughts become more balanced, emotions stabilize, and individuals often feel motivated to engage in positive behaviors, creating a feedback loop that supports mental health improvement.

4. Techniques Used in CBT for Depression

CBT offers various structured techniques tailored to address the specific challenges of depression. Some of the most commonly used techniques include:

- Cognitive Restructuring: This technique involves identifying "cognitive distortions" – irrational and exaggerated thought patterns common in depression, such as black-and-white thinking or catastrophizing. For example, a person might think, "I always fail," after one minor setback. Cognitive restructuring helps patients recognize these distortions and replace them with more balanced, realistic thoughts.

- Behavioral Activation: Depressed individuals often avoid activities they used to enjoy. Behavioral activation encourages them to participate in these activities again, even if they don't feel motivated. This technique recognizes that engaging in positive actions can eventually improve mood.

- Journaling and Thought Records: Patients are encouraged to keep a journal where they document their thoughts, feelings, and behaviors. By regularly reviewing these entries with a therapist, individuals gain insights into patterns of negative thinking and learn to challenge these thoughts.

- Exposure Therapy: For those who also experience anxiety or fear associated with depression, exposure therapy gradually introduces them to anxiety-provoking situations. By doing so, they build confidence and resilience, reducing avoidance behaviors.

- Mindfulness and Relaxation Techniques: CBT often incorporates mindfulness, where individuals learn to observe their thoughts non-judgmentally and stay grounded in the present moment. Relaxation techniques, such as deep breathing or progressive muscle relaxation, also help reduce physical symptoms of anxiety and depression.

5. How CBT Helps Combat Depression

CBT's effectiveness in treating depression lies in its structured approach to identifying and changing the negative thoughts and behaviors that fuel depressive symptoms. Here are some specific ways CBT combats depression:

- Breaking the Cycle of Negative Thinking: Depression often involves repetitive negative thoughts that reinforce low mood. By addressing these thoughts, CBT helps individuals break free from a cycle of rumination and self-criticism.

- Encouraging Positive Behavioral Change: Depression can cause individuals to withdraw from activities, which worsens feelings of isolation and sadness. Behavioral activation in CBT encourages individuals to engage in meaningful activities, which can uplift mood and promote a sense of accomplishment.

- Empowering Self-Awareness: Through techniques like thought monitoring, CBT helps individuals become more aware of their thinking patterns and how these impact their emotions. This self-awareness is empowering and helps patients develop coping skills to manage future depressive episodes.

- Building Problem-Solving Skills: Depression often makes it difficult to cope with stressors, leading to feelings of helplessness. CBT's focus on problem-solving equips individuals with practical tools to tackle challenges, reducing stress and enhancing resilience.

- Reducing Avoidance Behaviors: Depression frequently leads to avoidance of responsibilities or social interactions, which worsens isolation. CBT helps patients confront and overcome these avoidance behaviors, allowing them to rebuild relationships and regain a sense of purpose.

6. Evidence for the Effectiveness of CBT in Treating Depression

Numerous studies support CBT as an effective treatment for depression. Research has consistently shown that CBT can:

- Reduce Symptoms of Depression: CBT has been proven to reduce the severity of depressive symptoms, with many individuals experiencing significant improvement within 12-20 sessions.

- Prevent Relapse: CBT equips individuals with long-term coping skills, making it less likely they'll experience relapse compared to some other therapies. Studies suggest that CBT can help patients remain depression-free for extended periods, even after therapy has ended.

- Work for Diverse Populations: CBT has been effective across age groups, from children to older adults, and has also shown promising results in treating a range of depression types, including major depressive disorder and postpartum depression.

7. Practical Steps to Integrate CBT Strategies in Daily Life

To apply CBT principles, individuals can integrate the following practices into their daily routines:

- Identify and Challenge Negative Thoughts: Start by writing down negative thoughts when they occur. Ask yourself questions like, "Is this thought accurate?" or "What evidence supports or contradicts this thought?"

- Set Small Goals: Depression often makes tasks feel overwhelming. Setting small, manageable goals can help create momentum and a sense of accomplishment.

- Engage in Positive Activities: Choose one or two activities each day that you enjoy or value, and commit to doing them, even if motivation is low.

- Practice Mindfulness: Focus on being present in the moment, observing thoughts without judgment, and grounding yourself with deep breathing exercises.

- Reframe Situations: When encountering stress or disappointment, practice reframing by asking, "How else could I view this situation?" and look for positive or neutral interpretations.

Conclusion: Embracing CBT as a Path to Recovery

Cognitive Behavioral Therapy offers an empowering and practical approach to managing depression. By examining and reshaping thought patterns and behaviors, individuals can break free from the grip of depressive thinking, reclaim control, and cultivate resilience. Whether practiced in a therapeutic setting or integrated into daily life, CBT provides tools for emotional health, empowering individuals to confront challenges with greater self-awareness and confidence. As a result, they experience not only a reduction in depressive symptoms but also an enhanced quality of life rooted in resilience, hope, and inner peace.

Basic CBT Techniques for Self-Practice

Empowering Yourself Through Cognitive Behavioral Techniques

Introduction: The Value of Self-Practice in CBT

Cognitive Behavioral Therapy (CBT) is not only useful within a formal therapy setting but also as a self-help approach for managing negative thought patterns, enhancing emotional resilience, and addressing mood challenges. This chapter explores several foundational CBT techniques that can be practiced independently, empowering individuals to improve their mental well-being.

1. The Benefits of Self-Practiced CBT

Self-practicing CBT techniques offers several benefits. It allows individuals to:

- Identify and Challenge Negative Thoughts in real-time, leading to healthier thought patterns.

- Manage Stress and Anxiety by addressing unhelpful cognitive and behavioral responses.

- Promote Positive Behavioral Change by encouraging small, achievable steps.

- Gain Self-Awareness to better understand and manage emotional triggers.

By implementing these techniques consistently, individuals can experience greater control over their mental health.

2. Foundational Techniques for Self-Practice in CBT

Here are the essential CBT techniques that can be self-practiced, along with step-by-step guidance on implementing each.

A. Thought Journaling (Automatic Thought Record)

What It Is:

Thought journaling involves recording one's thoughts, particularly during moments of distress or intense emotions. The purpose is to identify and analyze recurring negative or irrational thoughts.

How to Implement Thought Journaling:

1. Recognize a Triggering Event: Whenever you feel a negative emotion, pause and identify the situation that triggered it.

2. Write Down Your Automatic Thoughts: Record the initial thoughts that surfaced in response to the event. This could be any negative thought, belief, or assumption.

3. Identify Associated Emotions: Write down the feelings tied to these thoughts and rate the intensity on a scale from 1 to 10.

4. Challenge and Reframe the Thoughts: After acknowledging your automatic thoughts, ask yourself if they're entirely accurate. Are there other perspectives you could consider? Write down alternative, more balanced thoughts.

5. Observe Emotional Shifts: Re-rate your emotional intensity after reframing. Often, more balanced thinking can reduce the intensity of negative feelings.

Example Entry:

- Trigger: My friend didn't respond to my text.

- Automatic Thought: "They're ignoring me; they probably don't like me anymore."

- Emotion: Anxiety, sadness (8/10)

- Reframed Thought: "Maybe they're busy, or they didn't see my message. There could be multiple reasons for the delay."

- New Emotion Rating: Anxiety, sadness (4/10)

Thought journaling helps to challenge negative thinking patterns, allowing for a healthier response to situations.

B. Cognitive Restructuring

What It Is:

Cognitive restructuring is the process of identifying and changing cognitive distortions—unrealistic and unhelpful thought patterns like catastrophizing, overgeneralization, and "all-or-nothing" thinking.

How to Implement Cognitive Restructuring:

1. Identify the Cognitive Distortion: Recognize when you're engaging in an unhelpful thought pattern.

2. Examine the Evidence: Ask yourself what objective evidence supports or contradicts the thought. Are you focusing only on the negatives?

3. Reframe the Thought: Replace the distortion with a more balanced perspective. For example, replace "I'll never succeed" with "I didn't succeed this time, but I can learn and improve."

4. Observe the Impact on Mood: Notice how reframing affects your mood and any urge to take different actions.

Example Cognitive Distortions:

- All-or-Nothing Thinking: Viewing things in black-or-white terms, e.g., "I failed this task, so I'm a failure."

- Catastrophizing: Assuming the worst possible outcome will happen.

- Mind Reading: Believing you know what others think about you without evidence.

Cognitive restructuring is essential for breaking the cycle of irrational thoughts that fuel negative emotions.

C. Behavioral Activation

What It Is:

Behavioral activation is the practice of scheduling and engaging in positive activities that improve mood and motivation. Depression can often lead to inactivity, which worsens feelings of isolation and hopelessness.

How to Implement Behavioral Activation:

1. Identify Avoided Activities: List activities you used to enjoy or know are beneficial (e.g., exercising, hobbies, socializing).

2. Set Small Goals: Start with small, manageable goals to prevent feeling overwhelmed. For instance, "Take a 10-minute walk" instead of "Exercise for an hour."

3. Plan and Schedule: Put these activities on your calendar to create accountability.

4. Reflect on the Outcome: After completing an activity, take note of any improvements in mood or energy, even if subtle. Recognize and reinforce these positive effects.

Behavioral activation encourages individuals to take proactive steps toward mental wellness by re-engaging with activities that foster positive emotions.

D. Exposure Therapy (Facing Fears Gradually)

What It Is:

Exposure therapy is a CBT technique often used for anxiety and avoidance behaviors. The goal is to confront feared situations gradually to reduce anxiety.

How to Implement Exposure Therapy:

1. Identify Your Fear Hierarchy: List situations you avoid due to fear, ranking them from least to most anxiety-provoking.

2. Start Small: Begin with the least threatening situation and gradually work your way up.

3. Stay in the Situation Until Anxiety Decreases: Allow yourself to experience the discomfort until it naturally

declines. Avoiding the situation can reinforce fear, but facing it reduces anxiety over time.

4. Celebrate Small Wins: Recognize and reward yourself for confronting each fear, no matter how small.

This method teaches the mind that feared situations are not as threatening as they seem, leading to a decrease in avoidance behaviors and ultimately improving confidence and mood.

E. Mindfulness and Relaxation Techniques

What It Is:

Mindfulness involves focusing on the present moment without judgment, which helps individuals detach from overwhelming thoughts and emotions. Relaxation techniques, such as deep breathing and progressive muscle relaxation, complement mindfulness by reducing physical tension associated with anxiety and stress.

How to Practice Mindfulness and Relaxation:

1. Deep Breathing: Inhale slowly, filling your belly with air, then exhale completely. Repeat several times to calm the mind.

2. Progressive Muscle Relaxation: Tense and relax each muscle group, starting from your toes and working your way up.

3. Mindfulness Meditation: Sit quietly and focus on your breath. If your mind wanders, gently bring your attention back to your breath. This builds resilience against intrusive thoughts.

4. Body Scan: Mentally scan each part of your body, noting any tension or sensations. Practicing this regularly helps release physical stress.

Mindfulness and relaxation techniques are especially beneficial for managing anxiety and creating a sense of calm.

F. Goal Setting and Problem-Solving

What It Is:

Goal setting and problem-solving are CBT strategies that help individuals address obstacles in a structured way, promoting feelings of accomplishment and reducing overwhelm.

How to Implement Goal Setting and Problem-Solving:

1. Set Specific, Realistic Goals: Break down large goals into smaller, achievable tasks. Make sure each goal is SMART (Specific, Measurable, Achievable, Relevant, and Time-bound).

2. Identify Obstacles: List potential obstacles to achieving your goal.

3. Develop Solutions: Brainstorm possible solutions for each obstacle, aiming for practical and achievable approaches.

4. Track Progress: Regularly check in on your goals, celebrate progress, and adjust as needed.

Problem-solving helps reduce the helplessness often associated with depression by equipping individuals to take control of challenging situations.

3. Integrating CBT Techniques into Daily Life

To benefit from CBT techniques, consistency is key. Here are some tips for integrating these practices into your daily routine:

- Set Aside Time for Self-Practice: Dedicate at least 10-15 minutes a day to practicing one of these techniques.

- Monitor Your Progress: Keep a log of your thought records, exposure steps, and goal achievements to observe your growth.

- Seek Support if Needed: While self-practice is empowering, it can be helpful to seek guidance from a therapist when dealing with complex emotions or setbacks.

Conclusion: Empowering Self-Practice with CBT

Practicing CBT techniques independently can significantly enhance mental well-being by fostering healthier thought patterns and actions. While challenging at first, these practices gradually build resilience, helping individuals manage depression and anxiety more effectively. With regular self-practice, these foundational techniques encourage lasting change, empowering individuals to take charge of their mental health journey.

Theological Reflections on Mind Renewal

Renewing the Mind: A Spiritual Foundation for Overcoming Destructive Thoughts

Introduction: The Significance of Mind Renewal in Faith

The concept of renewing the mind is central to Christian theology and personal transformation. Rooted in biblical teachings, renewing the mind involves replacing destructive, negative thoughts with truth and aligning one's mindset with God's will and wisdom. This process isn't merely about thinking positively; it is a profound spiritual practice that allows believers to live according to the truth of God's Word, foster emotional well-being, and combat the destructive thoughts that can lead to depression, anxiety, and despair.

The Apostle Paul emphasizes the importance of mind renewal, urging believers, "Do not conform to the pattern of this world, but be transformed by the renewing of your mind.

Then you will be able to test and approve what God's will is—his good, pleasing, and perfect will" (Romans 12:2, NIV). This passage highlights the transformative power of aligning one's thoughts with divine truths as a foundation for spiritual growth and mental resilience.

1. The Importance of Renewing the Mind According to Scripture

Throughout Scripture, the mind is recognized as a vital battleground where spiritual and psychological conflicts are often waged. The Bible teaches that the state of our mind affects our character, actions, and overall spiritual health. Renewing the mind is therefore not only encouraged but also necessary for believers to:

- Discern God's Will: Renewing the mind helps us understand and follow God's will, as seen in Romans 12:2.

- Overcome Temptation: Guarding our thoughts with truth helps resist worldly influences and temptations.

- Maintain Inner Peace: Negative thoughts, if left unchecked, can lead to unrest, while godly thinking fosters peace (Philippians 4:8-9).

2. Biblical Examples of Mind Renewal and Transformation

The Bible provides numerous examples of individuals who experienced transformation by renewing their minds and trusting in God's truth.

A. King David: Replacing Despair with Hope in God

David frequently faced trials, from the betrayal of friends to threats on his life. In Psalm 42:5, David speaks to himself, saying, "Why, my soul, are you downcast? Why so disturbed within me? Put your hope in God, for I will yet praise him, my Savior and my God." Here, David actively combats despair by focusing his mind on God's faithfulness and promises, reminding himself of the hope he has in God. This self-reflection and redirection illustrate mind renewal in action, showing the importance of shifting focus from circumstances to God's unchanging nature.

B. The Prodigal Son: Reclaiming Identity and Worth

The story of the prodigal son (Luke 15:11-32) shows a young man who, after losing everything, renews his mind by remembering his father's love and forgiveness. In a moment of clarity, he decides to return to his father's house, reflecting a restored sense of worth and trust in his father's mercy. This decision marks a turning point, as he moves from guilt and shame to reconciliation and restoration. His journey illustrates how renewing one's mind with thoughts of God's grace can lead to healing and renewed purpose.

C. The Apostle Paul: Finding Contentment and Joy

Paul, while imprisoned, wrote, "I have learned to be content whatever the circumstances" (Philippians 4:11). Paul's contentment was rooted in his renewal of mind—he focused not on his hardships but on God's strength and faithfulness. In Philippians 4:8, Paul encourages believers to meditate on things that are "true, noble, right, pure, lovely, admirable," which reflects a disciplined practice of replacing negative thoughts with uplifting truths.

3. How the Practice of Mind Renewal Helps Overcome Destructive Thoughts

A. Recognizing Destructive Thoughts

Destructive thoughts are any thoughts that go against God's truth, diminishing one's sense of worth, purpose, or hope. According to 2 Corinthians 10:5, believers are called to "take captive every thought to make it obedient to Christ." This means actively identifying and rejecting thoughts that lead to discouragement, fear, or hopelessness. Recognizing destructive thoughts is the first step to overcoming them and replacing them with scriptural truths.

B. Replacing Lies with Biblical Truth

Once destructive thoughts are identified, the next step is to replace them with God's truth. Jesus taught that "the truth will set you free" (John 8:32), emphasizing the liberating power of truth. For instance:

- If one struggles with thoughts of unworthiness, they can reflect on Ephesians 2:10, which says, "For we are God's masterpiece. He has created us anew in Christ Jesus, so we can do the good things he planned for us long ago."

- For those facing fear, recalling Isaiah 41:10—"So do not fear, for I am with you; do not be dismayed, for I am your God"—provides reassurance of God's presence.

By aligning one's thoughts with these truths, negative beliefs lose their power, fostering a healthier, God-centered mindset.

4. Practical Steps for Mind Renewal

Renewing the mind is a daily practice that involves consistent, faith-based actions. Here are some strategies for cultivating this habit.

A. Meditating on Scripture

Meditating on Scripture is a powerful way to internalize God's Word. Joshua 1:8 instructs believers to "keep this Book of the Law always on your lips; meditate on it day and night, so that you may be careful to do everything written in it." Through consistent meditation, the mind becomes more aligned with God's teachings, making it easier to replace destructive thoughts with uplifting truths.

B. Prayer and Surrender

Prayer is a means of connecting with God, presenting one's thoughts and concerns to Him, and inviting His wisdom. Philippians 4:6-7 reminds us, "Do not be anxious about anything, but in every situation, by prayer and petition, with thanksgiving, present your requests to God. And the peace of God…will guard your hearts and your minds in Christ Jesus." Prayer can create peace by surrendering worries to God, which renews and restores the mind.

C. Practicing Gratitude

Focusing on gratitude can shift the mind from a perspective of lack to one of abundance. According to 1 Thessalonians 5:18, "give thanks in all circumstances; for this is God's will for you in Christ Jesus." Gratitude reduces the inclination toward negativity, promoting mental clarity and resilience against depressive thoughts.

D. Choosing Positive Associations

1 Corinthians 15:33 warns, "Do not be misled: 'Bad company corrupts good character.'" Surrounding oneself with positive, faith-centered individuals encourages a supportive environment for mind renewal. By engaging with people who speak truth, hope, and encouragement, individuals are more likely to maintain a spiritually sound and resilient mindset.

5. The Impact of Mind Renewal on Mental Health and Spiritual Growth

When one consistently renews the mind with God's truth, it becomes possible to experience greater peace, joy, and purpose. This alignment with God's wisdom serves as a shield against negative thought patterns that can lead to emotional and mental distress.

Mind renewal not only enhances mental well-being but also strengthens one's faith journey. With a mind centered on God's promises, believers can approach life's challenges with courage and confidence, secure in their identity as children of God.

Conclusion: Embracing the Transformation of Mind Renewal

The call to renew the mind is both a command and a promise of transformation. By committing to this practice, believers can experience freedom from destructive thoughts and align themselves with God's will. Through daily meditation, prayer, gratitude, and intentional associations, mind renewal becomes a source of strength and hope, allowing one to live a life rooted in God's truth.

As Romans 12:2 urges, "Be transformed by the renewing of your mind." This transformation is the essence of spiritual growth and the foundation of a life filled with peace, purpose, and resilience.

CHAPTER 11

ELECTROCONVULSIVE THERAPY (ETC)

Introduction: The Role of Electroconvulsive Therapy in Mental Health

Electroconvulsive Therapy (ECT) is a medical treatment primarily used for individuals with severe, treatment-resistant depression. ECT involves the application of controlled electrical currents to the brain while the patient is under general anesthesia, resulting in a brief, controlled seizure. This treatment has been both a topic of intrigue and misconception, often due to historical misuse or dramatization in media. However, when administered under modern guidelines, ECT is a highly controlled, safe, and often effective method for alleviating severe depressive symptoms, particularly in patients who do not respond to other treatments.

1. What is Electroconvulsive Therapy?

ECT was first introduced in the 1930s as a therapeutic option for severe psychiatric disorders, and despite evolving opinions and approaches, it remains a part of modern psychiatry. ECT is specifically designed to address cases where other treatments, such as medications and psychotherapy, have not been successful. During ECT, a small, controlled amount of electrical current is passed through the brain, inducing a brief seizure that alters the brain's chemical balance.

The exact mechanism by which ECT relieves symptoms of depression is not fully understood, but studies suggest that it leads to the release of neurotransmitters—chemicals like serotonin, dopamine, and norepinephrine—associated with mood regulation. By inducing these changes, ECT can offer relief from symptoms in a relatively short period, particularly useful for those at risk of self-harm or suicide due to severe depressive episodes.

2. How Does ECT Work?

ECT is administered in a medical setting by trained professionals, including psychiatrists and anesthesiologists. Here is an overview of the process:

1. Preparation and Anesthesia: Patients are first given a general anesthetic to ensure they remain unconscious during the procedure. They may also receive a muscle relaxant to prevent physical movement during the seizure.

2. Electrode Placement: Electrodes are placed on the patient's scalp, either unilaterally (on one side of the head) or bilaterally (on both sides).

3. Application of Electrical Current: A carefully controlled electrical current is passed through the electrodes, resulting in a brief seizure that typically lasts between 20 to 60 seconds.

4. Monitoring and Recovery: Patients are monitored closely throughout the procedure. After the seizure, they are taken to a recovery area until the effects of the anesthesia have worn off.

Each ECT session typically takes about 5-10 minutes, with the entire preparation and recovery process lasting about an hour. Most ECT treatment plans consist of multiple sessions over several weeks.

3. When is ECT Recommended?

ECT is generally recommended when other treatments for depression, such as medications or psychotherapy, have been ineffective. Common indications include:

- Treatment-Resistant Depression: ECT is often prescribed for patients who have not responded to at least two different antidepressant medications and/or adequate trials of psychotherapy.

- Severe Major Depressive Episodes: Patients experiencing intense symptoms, such as extreme suicidal ideation or catatonia, may benefit from the rapid symptom relief that ECT can provide.

- Bipolar Disorder: ECT can also be used to treat depressive or manic episodes in bipolar disorder, particularly when other treatments are ineffective.

- Psychotic Depression: Depression with psychotic features—such as hallucinations or delusions—often responds well to ECT, sometimes more so than to medication alone.

- Need for Rapid Response: In some cases, where there is a need for a fast therapeutic effect, such as in patients with high suicide risk, ECT may be considered due to its rapid onset of action compared to most antidepressants, which can take weeks to become fully effective.

4. Efficacy and Benefits of ECT

Studies show that ECT is one of the most effective treatments for severe, treatment-resistant depression, with success rates often ranging from 70% to 90% in these patients. Benefits of ECT include:

- Rapid Symptom Relief: Unlike most medications, which require several weeks to take effect, ECT can provide relief within days. This rapid action is crucial for individuals experiencing severe or life-threatening depression.

- Efficacy in Resistant Cases: ECT is particularly valuable for individuals who have not found relief through other methods, providing an alternative path to recovery.

- Positive Impact on Quality of Life: For patients whose daily functioning is impaired by depression, ECT can help restore a sense of normalcy, allowing them to engage in everyday activities again.

While ECT may not provide a permanent solution, it is often highly effective in alleviating symptoms during critical periods, potentially allowing other treatments to become more effective after initial symptom relief.

5. Side Effects and Risks Associated with ECT

Though ECT is generally safe, like any medical procedure, it carries some risks and potential side effects. The most common side effects include:

- Short-term Memory Loss: Some patients experience memory problems, particularly regarding events around the time of treatment. This is usually temporary, but in some cases, memory issues can persist.

- Headache and Nausea: After ECT, some patients report mild headaches or nausea, which can usually be managed with medication.

- Confusion: Immediately following the procedure, some patients experience confusion, which typically clears within an hour.

- Potential for Long-Term Memory Loss: Although rare, some patients may experience lasting memory loss, particularly when bilateral electrode placement is used.

Due to these risks, ECT is generally reserved for severe cases, where its benefits outweigh potential side effects. Careful monitoring and follow-up can also help manage any adverse effects.

6. Psychological and Social Impacts of ECT

ECT has unique psychological and social implications. Many patients experience a profound sense of relief as symptoms improve, leading to increased functionality and a better quality of life. However, the stigma associated with ECT, due to historical portrayals, can sometimes lead to fear or reluctance to pursue the treatment.

Studies indicate that when patients are well-informed about ECT and the potential outcomes, satisfaction rates are high. Family and social support play a significant role in this process, helping individuals make informed choices and cope with any lingering fears about the treatment.

7. Complementing ECT with Other Treatments

While ECT can provide significant relief, it is often used as part of a broader treatment plan that may include:

- Medication: Antidepressants or mood stabilizers can be prescribed following ECT to help maintain symptom relief.

- Psychotherapy: Therapy, such as Cognitive Behavioral Therapy (CBT), can complement ECT by helping individuals manage stressors and develop coping skills, which may reduce the need for future ECT sessions.

- Lifestyle Adjustments: Regular exercise, balanced nutrition, and adequate sleep can support overall mental health and reduce depressive symptoms, supplementing the effects of ECT.

For some individuals, ECT serves as a necessary intervention during a crisis, while for others, it may be part of a long-term management plan for chronic, treatment-resistant depression.

8. Ethical Considerations and Patient Rights

Due to the powerful effects of ECT, there are ethical guidelines to protect patient rights and ensure informed consent. Key ethical considerations include:

- Informed Consent: Patients must be provided with clear, accessible information about the procedure, potential side effects, and expected outcomes.

- Right to Refuse: Individuals have the right to decline ECT, and other options should be discussed.

- Patient-Centered Approach: Treatment plans should consider each individual's unique needs, values, and preferences, with family involvement where appropriate.

In cases where ECT is recommended, it is crucial to work with patients empathetically, addressing any concerns and ensuring a sense of empowerment throughout the process.

Conclusion: ECT as a Path to Hope and Healing

Electroconvulsive Therapy, when used appropriately, can be a life-saving intervention for individuals suffering from severe, treatment-resistant depression. Though often misunderstood, ECT offers hope to those who have not found relief through other means. With its potential for rapid symptom alleviation, ECT provides an option for patients to regain control of their lives and find a renewed sense of hope. Understanding ECT's role, benefits, and ethical considerations empowers patients and caregivers to make informed choices and fosters a compassionate, effective approach to mental health care.

Addressing Stigma and Misconceptions

Reassurance about the Safety and Efficacy of Electroconvulsive Therapy (ECT)

Introduction: Breaking Down Barriers to ECT

Electroconvulsive Therapy (ECT) is a powerful and effective treatment for severe depression and other mental health conditions, particularly in cases where other therapies have failed. Despite its efficacy, ECT is often underutilized due to lingering stigma and misconceptions surrounding the procedure. Popular media, past misuse, and lack of understanding have contributed to negative perceptions that can prevent patients from considering this potentially life-changing treatment. This chapter aims to address common myths and fears, provide reassurance about ECT's safety, and emphasize its value for individuals with treatment-resistant conditions.

1. Understanding the Origins of ECT Stigma

The stigma surrounding ECT largely stems from historical practices and dramatic portrayals in media. In its early days, ECT was often administered without anesthesia or proper monitoring, causing discomfort and fueling misconceptions about the treatment's safety and purpose. These outdated practices have long since been replaced by rigorous medical protocols, but memories of these past practices linger, influencing both public perception and individual decisions.

Popular media has also contributed to ECT's negative image. Films and television shows often depict ECT as a last-resort or punitive measure, portraying it as a painful and dehumanizing experience. This portrayal is not only inaccurate but detracts from the reality that modern ECT is a medically supervised, safe, and often highly effective treatment for severe depression, bipolar disorder, and certain other psychiatric conditions.

2. Addressing Common Misconceptions about ECT

Several misconceptions fuel the stigma surrounding ECT, including:

- Misconception 1: ECT is Painful and Violent

Contrary to common belief, modern ECT is performed under general anesthesia, meaning the patient is completely unconscious during the procedure and feels no pain. Patients receive a muscle relaxant to minimize any physical movement, making the procedure safe and controlled. The only sensation most patients experience afterward is mild grogginess or a slight headache, which quickly subsides.

- Misconception 2: ECT Causes Severe Memory Loss

While some memory effects can occur, especially with bilateral electrode placement, memory issues are typically mild and temporary. Most patients retain all long-term memories, with minor short-term memory disruption usually limited to the time surrounding the treatment period. Doctors today carefully monitor and adjust the treatment to minimize memory effects, and any persistent memory issues are relatively rare.

- Misconception 3: ECT is Only for "Severe Cases"

While ECT is generally reserved for individuals with severe or treatment-resistant conditions, it is not exclusively a last-resort treatment. For individuals experiencing significant distress or those at risk of suicide, ECT can provide quick relief, allowing them to stabilize and engage in other forms of therapy more effectively. This timely intervention is not about severity alone but about improving quality of life.

3. The Safety and Efficacy of ECT: Evidence and Reassurance

Modern ECT has been extensively studied, and its safety profile is well-established. Research shows that ECT can be significantly more effective than some other treatments for severe depression, especially when other methods have not yielded results. Key points regarding ECT's efficacy and safety include:

- High Success Rate: Studies indicate that ECT has success rates between 70-90% in alleviating symptoms of severe, treatment-resistant depression, often within a shorter time frame than other therapies.

- Minimal Physical Side Effects: Since ECT is conducted under general anesthesia with muscle relaxants, physical effects are mild and short-lived, with minimal discomfort or pain for the patient.

- Well-Established Protocols: ECT is performed in highly controlled settings by specialized medical professionals, ensuring that each treatment is carefully tailored to the patient's needs. Adjustments in electrode placement, current intensity, and session frequency help maximize effectiveness while minimizing side effects.

4. Why Stigma Persists: Psychological and Social Factors

Despite robust evidence supporting ECT's safety and effectiveness, stigma persists due to deep-rooted psychological and social factors. Patients may feel embarrassed or ashamed to consider ECT, worrying about how others will perceive them. Many people also harbor internalized fears due to the invasive nature of the treatment, mistakenly equating ECT with coercion or a loss of control over their mental health.

Social stigma around mental health in general further complicates perceptions of ECT. Even as attitudes towards mental illness become more compassionate, there remains a degree of fear and misunderstanding about psychiatric treatments, especially those that involve medical procedures.

This cultural backdrop influences patients and their families, creating barriers to considering ECT as a viable option for mental health recovery.

5. The Role of Education and Advocacy in Changing Perceptions

Education plays a crucial role in dismantling the stigma surrounding ECT. When patients, families, and mental health professionals have accurate information, they are better equipped to make informed decisions without the cloud of misconception. Advocacy by mental health organizations, medical professionals, and former ECT patients can help shift public perceptions by offering realistic portrayals and personal success stories.

- Patient Stories and Testimonials: Hearing directly from individuals who have benefited from ECT can humanize the treatment and provide hope for those considering it. Former patients can offer unique insights into how ECT transformed their lives, normalizing the treatment and encouraging others to seek help without shame.

- Medical and Professional Transparency: By explaining the treatment process, outcomes, and possible side effects in detail, healthcare providers can empower patients to make informed choices, reducing fear and uncertainty.

- Public Awareness Campaigns: Many mental health organizations work to dispel myths about ECT through public awareness campaigns. These campaigns aim to educate the public on the realities of ECT, emphasizing its effectiveness and the strict safety standards that govern its administration.

6. ECT as a Path to Recovery: Real-Life Benefits and Case Studies

ECT has changed many lives by offering individuals with severe mental health conditions a path to recovery. For patients with intractable depression, bipolar disorder, and psychotic features, ECT provides an alternative to continued suffering, allowing them to regain control over their lives. Real-life cases often demonstrate the positive impact of ECT:

- Rapid Symptom Relief: Many patients experience significant mood improvements within days, rather than weeks, helping them stabilize and begin participating in other therapeutic activities.

- Enhanced Engagement in Life: By alleviating symptoms, ECT enables individuals to reconnect with family, work, and social activities, enhancing overall quality of life.

- Reduction in Hospitalizations: For individuals frequently hospitalized due to psychiatric crises, ECT has been shown to reduce the need for emergency interventions, providing a stable baseline that reduces the frequency of hospital admissions.

Such cases demonstrate the profound impact ECT can have on individuals who had previously found limited relief from other therapies, offering a new sense of hope and possibility.

7. Encouraging Informed Decision-Making

Patients and families should be encouraged to approach ECT as one of many possible treatment options rather than as a measure of last resort. An informed decision-making process involves understanding:

- The Benefits of ECT: Familiarizing oneself with the success rates and potential improvements can help patients weigh ECT alongside other treatments.

- Personalized Care: Patients should discuss with their healthcare providers the specifics of ECT, including customized treatment plans that fit their individual needs and mental health history.

- Open Dialogue: Encouraging honest conversations with family members and loved ones can help reduce any shame or stigma, fostering a supportive environment for recovery.

Ultimately, the decision to undergo ECT should be one of empowerment rather than fear, grounded in understanding its potential to alleviate suffering and restore quality of life.

Conclusion: Embracing ECT as a Valid Treatment Option

ECT is a highly effective treatment for individuals facing severe, treatment-resistant depression and other psychiatric conditions, offering relief to those who have not benefited from traditional therapies. Addressing the stigma and misconceptions surrounding ECT is essential to ensure that individuals are aware of all available options and can make informed decisions in their mental health journey.

As education and open conversations about ECT continue to evolve, so too can the public's perception of this life-saving treatment. For patients who need it, ECT provides not only a renewed sense of well-being but also the hope that recovery is achievable. With greater awareness and support, ECT can be recognized not as a measure of last resort but as a powerful tool for healing in the fight against severe mental health disorders.

Theological Perspectives on Modern Medicine

Exploring the Acceptance of Medical Treatments within Religious Contexts

Introduction: Bridging Faith and Medicine

In many religious traditions, spirituality and physical well-being are deeply connected, as health is seen not only as the absence of disease but also as a state of wholeness and harmony with the divine. This holistic view suggests that medical treatments and spiritual practices are complementary rather than contradictory, supporting one another in the healing process. However, modern medicine has often focused on the physical and clinical aspects of health, sidelining the spiritual dimension of patient care.

Exploring how spirituality aligns with contemporary medical treatments reveals valuable insights about how faith and medicine can coexist, addressing both the soul and body of patients, especially during profound illnesses or mental health struggles.

1. The Role of Faith in Healing

Across various cultures and religious traditions, faith is viewed as an essential component of healing. In Christianity, for example, scripture portrays Jesus as both a healer of physical ailments and a restorer of the spirit. Stories of miraculous healings, such as Jesus curing blindness (John 9:1-7) or restoring a paralyzed man's mobility (Mark 2:1-12), emphasize that health restoration involves not only physical but also spiritual renewal.

For believers, trusting in God's healing power while seeking medical treatment reflects an understanding that all healing ultimately comes from God, whether it occurs through miraculous means or medical intervention. This belief fosters a sense of peace and acceptance, even during times of illness, as individuals feel their health is in divine hands.

2. The Overlap of Medicine and Spirituality

Studies have shown that spirituality plays a significant role in how patients cope with illness, and integrating spiritual care into medical treatment has led to positive outcomes in patient satisfaction, mental health, and pain management. Recognizing this, some healthcare providers and institutions have started incorporating spiritual care by providing chaplain services, counseling, and spaces for meditation and prayer.

Research indicates that patients often express a desire for their spiritual beliefs to be acknowledged during treatment. For example:

- Improved Coping Mechanisms: Patients who engage in spiritual practices, like prayer or meditation, often report a better ability to cope with pain and stress. This connection between spirituality and coping aligns with psychological theories that suggest practices fostering hope and purpose reduce emotional distress.

- Enhanced Resilience: Individuals with a strong spiritual foundation are often more resilient in the face of health challenges, as their faith helps them find meaning and purpose in their suffering. The belief in a higher purpose and divine plan provides comfort, reducing anxiety and depression, especially during terminal or chronic illness.

- Holistic Approach to Health: The spiritual dimension complements medical treatment by addressing emotional and existential questions, providing comfort that extends beyond physical healing. This holistic approach acknowledges that health is a multifaceted experience encompassing the mind, body, and spirit.

3. Spirituality and Medical Ethics: Embracing Medical Intervention

Religious teachings often affirm the role of medical intervention, viewing it as a manifestation of God's provision and wisdom given to humanity. For instance, in the Christian tradition, using medical treatment does not contradict faith in God; rather, it is seen as God working through skilled physicians and modern technology. Biblical references support the use of medicine and physicians, as seen in verses like:

- Jeremiah 8:22: "Is there no balm in Gilead? Is there no physician there? Why then has the health of the daughter of my people not been restored?" This verse implies that God acknowledges and supports the role of medicine in healing.

- Sirach 38:1-2: In the Apocryphal book of Sirach, it is written, "Honor physicians for their services, for the Lord created them; for their gift of healing comes from the Most High." This highlights the belief that physicians' skills are a gift from God, indicating that medical treatment aligns with divine will.

- Luke 10:34: The Good Samaritan cares for an injured man by pouring oil and wine on his wounds. This act of compassion, involving a type of medicinal treatment, symbolizes the practical, caring aspect of faith.

These passages emphasize that seeking medical care is not only acceptable but also encouraged, as it reflects gratitude for God-given resources and talents.

4. Addressing the Gap: Integrating Spiritual Care in Modern Medicine

Despite the benefits of integrating spirituality into healthcare, it remains a neglected aspect in many clinical settings. Physicians and medical professionals often receive little training in addressing spiritual needs, even though patients may experience spiritual distress alongside their physical symptoms. Addressing this gap requires:

- Training for Medical Professionals: Incorporating spirituality into medical education can prepare doctors, nurses, and other healthcare providers to recognize and respect patients' spiritual needs. This training can be practical, focusing on open, compassionate communication and familiarity with diverse faith traditions.

- Collaboration with Spiritual Leaders: Hospitals and clinics can collaborate with religious leaders to support patients' spiritual well-being, especially for those in palliative care or facing terminal illnesses. Chaplains and faith counselors can play an active role in this process, providing support that complements medical care.

- Encouraging Patient Autonomy: Allowing patients to share their spiritual beliefs without judgment empowers them to integrate faith into their treatment plans, which can lead to improved adherence to treatment and overall well-being.

5. Biblical Foundations of Mind Renewal and Healing

The concept of "renewing the mind" appears frequently in Christian scripture, particularly in addressing mental health and resilience. Romans 12:2 says, "Do not be conformed to this world, but be transformed by the renewal of your mind." This verse reflects a powerful theological perspective: mental renewal as a pathway to aligning one's mind with God's will, providing resilience against destructive thoughts and depression.

Similarly, Philippians 4:8 encourages believers to focus on "whatever is true, whatever is noble, whatever is right," promoting a mental shift toward positivity. When combined with therapeutic practices like Cognitive Behavioral Therapy (CBT), which aligns closely with the concept of "thought renewal," this biblical principle can enhance mental health recovery. Through both faith and therapy, individuals can learn to challenge negative thoughts, ultimately fostering a healthier mindset.

6. Faith and Mental Health: Spirituality as a Tool for Emotional Resilience

Spirituality offers unique tools for individuals coping with mental health challenges. Prayer, meditation, and community support are integral aspects of religious life that align with therapeutic practices shown to improve mental health. Evidence demonstrates that individuals who regularly engage in spiritual practices experience:

- Reduced Anxiety and Depression: Belief in a higher power often instills a sense of peace and purpose that helps reduce symptoms of anxiety and depression. Through prayer or meditation, individuals find a quiet space to reflect, experience gratitude, and connect with God, relieving mental distress.

- Strength in Community: Religious communities offer fellowship, helping individuals avoid isolation and creating a support network that fosters accountability and empathy.

- Purpose Beyond Suffering: Faith provides a framework for understanding and accepting suffering, allowing individuals to find purpose even in hardship. This belief can be particularly therapeutic for those dealing with chronic illness or life-altering conditions.

7. Practical Ways to Foster Spirituality in Medical Settings

For healthcare providers and institutions looking to honor patients' spirituality, several practical approaches can support a holistic experience:

- Incorporate Spiritual Assessments: Asking patients about their beliefs and values as part of intake can set the foundation for a respectful, personalized treatment plan.

- Provide Spaces for Prayer and Reflection: Designated spaces in hospitals for meditation and prayer can offer comfort, especially for patients in prolonged treatments.

- Offer Access to Chaplains or Faith Counselors: By facilitating chaplain visits, hospitals ensure that patients' spiritual needs are as respected as their medical needs.

Conclusion: Embracing Holistic Health through Faith and Medicine

Medicine and spirituality can coexist harmoniously, offering a complete approach to healing that respects both body and soul. While medical treatment focuses on curing illness, spirituality addresses the deeper questions of purpose, hope, and resilience. For people of faith, understanding that medical advancements and spiritual practices can work together to bring healing is empowering. This holistic approach enriches the patient experience and acknowledges the complexity of human health, bridging the gap between faith and science.

CHAPTER 12

SPIRITUAL PRACTICES IN OVERCOMING DEPRESSION

Prayer, Meditation, and Worship

Introduction: The Role of Spiritual Practices in Mental Health

In times of difficulty, spiritual practices such as prayer, meditation, and worship offer more than comfort; they provide grounding, stability, and peace. When dealing with depression, these practices can serve as powerful tools for healing, offering hope and clarity amidst the confusion and despair that often accompany mental illness. While therapeutic interventions like counseling and medication are essential, incorporating spiritual practices can add a meaningful dimension, helping individuals reconnect with a deeper sense of purpose and guidance.

1. Prayer as a Path to Inner Peace

Prayer is an age-old spiritual practice that serves as a direct line of communication with the divine. For those dealing with depression, prayer can provide a sense of relief and comfort by allowing them to express their deepest concerns, fears, and desires to a loving, understanding presence. Through prayer, many people feel they are not alone in their suffering but are accompanied by God, who listens and cares.

The Power of Surrender in Prayer

Prayer encourages surrender—a relinquishing of personal control and a willingness to trust in God's wisdom. For those facing depression, this act of surrender can be incredibly freeing, allowing them to release burdens too heavy to bear alone. Psalm 55:22 offers a powerful reminder: "Cast your cares on the Lord, and he will sustain you; he will never let the righteous be shaken." The act of laying down one's burdens in prayer often leads to a release of emotional and mental tension, fostering a sense of relief and peace.

Different Forms of Prayer

Prayer is versatile and can be practiced in various forms, each with its unique benefits:

- Intercessory Prayer: Praying for others often brings perspective, shifting focus from one's own suffering to the well-being of others.

- Thanksgiving Prayer: Expressing gratitude for blessings fosters a positive outlook, combating the negative thought patterns commonly associated with depression.

- Contemplative Prayer: This form involves meditative silence, centering on God's presence. It is often profoundly calming and restorative, creating mental stillness that helps ease anxiety.

2. Meditation as a Tool for Mental Clarity

Meditation is another spiritual practice that has been shown to have significant mental health benefits. While rooted in various religious traditions, meditation is adaptable to any belief system, focusing primarily on mindfulness and stillness. For people with depression, meditation offers an opportunity to quiet the mind and reduce the noise of negative thoughts that can be overwhelming.

Biblical Perspectives on Meditation

The Bible encourages meditation as a way to deepen one's relationship with God and find inner peace. In Psalm 1:2, meditation is described as delighting "in the law of the Lord, and on his law he meditates day and night." This practice allows individuals to connect more deeply with scripture, finding comfort and guidance in God's word.

Benefits of Meditation for Depression

Meditation has scientifically proven effects on mental well-being, helping to regulate mood and reduce stress. Benefits include:

- Increased Mindfulness: Meditation brings awareness to the present moment, reducing rumination on past regrets or anxieties about the future.

- Improved Emotional Regulation: Meditation trains the mind to observe thoughts without judgment, leading to better control over emotions and reduced impulsivity.

- Enhanced Relaxation: Deep breathing exercises often used in meditation trigger the body's relaxation response, decreasing heart rate and stress hormone levels.

For someone battling depression, this meditative grounding can bring moments of clarity and stillness, restoring balance to an overwhelmed mind.

3. Worship as an Expression of Faith and Connection

Worship goes beyond personal prayer or meditation; it is often a communal act of honoring God, whether through song, praise, or ritual. In the context of mental health, worship connects individuals with their faith communities and allows them to experience joy and gratitude through acts of devotion. Engaging in worship provides a profound sense of belonging, which is essential for people experiencing isolation due to depression.

Biblical Stories of Worship in Times of Struggle

Throughout the Bible, there are stories of worship during times of adversity. One example is the story of Paul and Silas, who, while imprisoned, sang hymns of worship to God despite their circumstances (Acts 16:25). Their worship not only brought comfort to themselves but also impacted others around them. This story teaches that worship can be a source of strength, shifting focus from despair to gratitude and hope.

Benefits of Worship for Mental Health

- Community Support: Worship in a communal setting creates bonds with others who share similar beliefs, providing emotional support and encouragement.

- Renewed Sense of Purpose: Worshiping a higher power brings individuals closer to their values and beliefs, helping to create a purpose that transcends personal challenges.

- Emotional Release: The act of singing or participating in worship can be cathartic, allowing for the release of pent-up emotions, whether joy, sadness, or gratitude.

4. How Spiritual Practices Foster a Sense of Stability and Purpose

One of the most challenging aspects of depression is the loss of direction and hope. Spiritual practices restore a sense of stability by fostering a connection to something greater. As individuals engage in prayer, meditation, and worship, they often experience a renewed sense of identity and belonging, which counteracts feelings of purposelessness.

Finding Purpose through Faith

Theological perspectives on purpose emphasize that each person's life holds intrinsic value and meaning. Jeremiah 29:11 reassures believers, saying, "For I know the plans I have for you, declares the Lord, plans for welfare and not for evil, to give you a future and a hope." This promise of divine purpose helps individuals anchor their lives in a perspective that transcends the ups and downs of mental health struggles.

A Path to Making Decisions Aligned with Faith

Spiritual practices provide clarity, helping people make decisions that align with their beliefs. This process of discernment can be life-affirming and protective, guiding individuals toward choices that support their well-being. For instance, someone who feels called to seek help through counseling or community support may find encouragement in Proverbs 11:14, which says, "Where there is no guidance, a people falls, but in an abundance of counselors there is safety." Such verses remind believers that seeking support is not only acceptable but wise.

5. Practical Steps to Incorporate Spiritual Practices Daily

For those seeking to integrate spiritual practices into their daily routines, a few practical steps can make these practices more accessible:

- Establish a Morning Prayer Routine: Beginning each day with prayer sets a positive tone, grounding the individual in gratitude and purpose.

- Set Aside Quiet Time for Meditation: Even a few minutes of silence each day can help clear the mind and bring peace.

- Participate in Worship Weekly: Whether attending church services or engaging in personal worship, regular acts of devotion create consistency and community.

- Keep a Prayer or Gratitude Journal: Writing down prayers or moments of gratitude can help reinforce positive thinking patterns and remind individuals of God's presence in their lives.

6. Research on the Impact of Spiritual Practices on Mental Health

Numerous studies affirm that spiritual practices positively affect mental health, reducing symptoms of depression and anxiety. Research has shown that regular prayer and meditation improve psychological resilience and reduce the frequency and severity of depressive episodes.

These practices contribute to a mindset of acceptance, reducing the power of intrusive, negative thoughts.

- Harvard University Studies: Research by Harvard Medical School highlights that prayer and meditation stimulate the brain's relaxation response, reducing stress and anxiety.

- Mayo Clinic Findings: The Mayo Clinic reports that prayer and spiritual connection positively influence health outcomes, both physically and mentally, by fostering a sense of peace and purpose.

Conclusion: Embracing Spirituality as a Foundation for Healing

Incorporating spiritual practices such as prayer, meditation, and worship into one's daily life can be transformative, particularly for individuals experiencing depression. These practices serve as a source of strength, grounding, and stability, providing comfort in times of darkness and uncertainty. Through connection with a higher power, individuals can experience a profound sense of peace, knowing they are supported and valued.

In the words of Philippians 4:6-7: "Do not be anxious about anything, but in every situation, by prayer and petition, with thanksgiving, present your requests to God. And the peace of God, which transcends all understanding, will guard your hearts and your minds in Christ Jesus." This promise encapsulates the essence of spiritual practices in healing: they are not merely rituals but a pathway to divine peace that sustains and restores.

Forgiveness and Letting Go

The Role of Forgiveness in Releasing Mental Burdens

Introduction: The Power of Forgiveness

Forgiveness is often described as an act of mercy and a path toward inner freedom. It involves releasing resentment, bitterness, and the desire for revenge. For many, forgiveness is both challenging and transformative, a spiritual journey as well as a psychological process. Letting go of past grievances can alleviate heavy mental and emotional burdens, clearing space for healing, peace, and resilience. Emerging research supports forgiveness as essential for psychological well-being, as it promotes healthier relationships and fosters a balanced outlook on life.

1. What is Forgiveness?

Forgiveness is the conscious decision to release feelings of anger, resentment, or vengeance toward someone who has harmed you, regardless of whether they "deserve" it. This act does not necessarily mean reconciling with the person or condoning their actions. Rather, forgiveness is about freeing oneself from the emotional weight of past hurts and moving forward with a sense of peace.

Biblical Understanding of Forgiveness

The Bible presents forgiveness as an essential component of a faithful life. Colossians 3:13 (KJV) instructs, "Forgive as the Lord forgave you," which highlights forgiveness as a divine mandate. Strong's Concordance shows that the Greek word for forgiveness, "aphesis," implies a letting go or release, which captures the essence of freeing oneself from past wrongs. This spiritual release reflects God's own act of grace toward humanity, inspiring believers to model this forgiveness in their own lives.

2. The Psychology of Forgiveness

Psychologists view forgiveness as a complex, multidimensional process that has been shown to have significant mental and physical health benefits. Forgiveness alleviates stress, reduces anxiety, and promotes emotional stability. Dr. Everett Worthington, a psychologist known for his research on forgiveness, has noted that forgiving others leads to lower blood pressure, reduced stress hormone levels, and improved immune function.

Research on Forgiveness and Health

Research highlights the profound impact of forgiveness on well-being. In a landmark study at Stanford University, participants who underwent forgiveness training reported significantly lower levels of stress, anger, and depression. These findings are supported by further research published in the Journal of Behavioral Medicine, which shows that forgiveness reduces symptoms of depression, anxiety, and stress, thus fostering mental and emotional resilience.

Positive Impact on Physical Health

Forgiveness affects not only mental but also physical health. Persistent anger and resentment trigger the body's stress response, releasing cortisol and other stress hormones that, over time, can lead to high blood pressure, cardiovascular issues, and immune suppression. By letting go of these negative emotions, people who practice forgiveness often report fewer physical ailments and a greater sense of physical well-being.

3. Biblical Stories of Forgiveness

Throughout the Bible, forgiveness is depicted as a path to divine peace and inner transformation. Several stories exemplify the profound power of forgiveness:

Joseph and His Brothers

The story of Joseph is one of the most powerful narratives on forgiveness in the Bible. Despite being betrayed and sold into slavery by his brothers, Joseph ultimately forgives them, saying in Genesis 50:20 (KJV), "But as for you, ye thought evil against me; but God meant it unto good." This act of forgiveness not only healed his family but also demonstrated how forgiveness can transform pain into purpose, showing that forgiveness often brings about reconciliation and restoration.

The Parable of the Prodigal Son

In the Parable of the Prodigal Son (Luke 15:11-32), Jesus illustrates forgiveness as an act of unconditional love. When the wayward son returns, the father welcomes him with open arms, symbolizing God's boundless grace. This parable underscores that forgiveness can bring healing and renewal, helping both the forgiver and the forgiven.

Jesus on the Cross

Perhaps the most powerful example of forgiveness is Jesus' words on the cross: "Father, forgive them; for they know not what they do" (Luke 23:34 KJV). Here, Jesus demonstrates that forgiveness is an act of compassion and strength, even in the face of intense suffering. This selfless act emphasizes that forgiveness is central to the Christian faith and highlights the redemptive power of letting go of bitterness.

4. How Forgiveness Benefits Mental Health

Forgiveness has become an area of interest in psychology because of its mental health benefits. By letting go of resentment, individuals can experience relief from symptoms of depression, anxiety, and PTSD. Dr. Robert

Enright, a leading researcher in the psychology of forgiveness, has demonstrated that forgiveness therapy helps people overcome traumatic experiences, reduce psychological stress, and improve emotional well-being.

Breaking the Cycle of Rumination

Forgiveness interrupts the cycle of rumination—repeatedly revisiting painful memories and negative thoughts—which is a significant contributor to depression and anxiety. By choosing to forgive, people can break free from these mental loops, freeing their minds to focus on positive growth.

Enhancing Resilience and Emotional Stability

Forgiveness fosters emotional resilience by helping individuals develop healthier coping mechanisms. Studies published in the Personality and Social Psychology Bulletin reveal that people who forgive others tend to have higher self-esteem, better conflict resolution skills, and a greater ability to manage negative emotions.

5. Forgiveness from a Theological Perspective: A Divine Mandate

Forgiveness is not only beneficial for mental health but is also a core tenet of many religious beliefs. In Christianity, forgiveness is seen as a divine mandate, an expression of God's nature that believers are called to emulate. Ephesians 4:32 (KJV) teaches, "And be ye kind one to another, tenderhearted, forgiving one another, even as God for Christ's sake hath forgiven you."

The Spiritual Liberation of Forgiveness

Forgiveness in the Bible is seen as an act of love and grace that liberates both the forgiver and the forgiven. By choosing to forgive, believers align themselves with God's will, freeing themselves from bitterness and opening their hearts to love and compassion.

Forgiveness as a Path to Spiritual Growth

Through forgiveness, individuals can draw closer to God, allowing them to transcend earthly grievances and focus on divine love. The act of forgiveness is a transformative process that refines character, cultivates patience, and fosters empathy—qualities that are essential to spiritual growth.

6. Practical Steps for Practicing Forgiveness

Forgiveness is a journey that requires intentionality, patience, and often divine guidance. For those seeking to practice forgiveness, here are some practical steps:

Reflect on Your Motives

Consider why you want to forgive. Are you seeking personal peace, spiritual growth, or reconciliation? By clarifying your motives, you can approach forgiveness from a place of authenticity.

Pray for Strength and Guidance

Prayer is a powerful tool that can provide strength and guidance in the process of forgiveness. Ask God for help in releasing bitterness and opening your heart to compassion.

Practice Empathy

Try to understand the other person's perspective. While this may be challenging, practicing empathy can help soften feelings of anger and resentment, making forgiveness more achievable.

Let Go of Expectations

Forgiveness does not require an apology from the other person or reconciliation. True forgiveness is an internal process that allows you to release negative emotions, regardless of the other person's response.

7. Research on Forgiveness Interventions and Therapeutic Techniques

Recent studies have highlighted the effectiveness of forgiveness interventions in clinical psychology. These techniques often include empathy-building exercises, self-reflection, and cognitive restructuring, all of which help individuals reframe past hurts and find closure.

Forgiveness Therapy

Forgiveness therapy, developed by Dr. Robert Enright, focuses on helping individuals confront their pain, cultivate empathy, and let go of resentment. This approach has been effective in reducing symptoms of PTSD, anxiety, and depression.

Self-Compassion and Forgiveness

Forgiving oneself is also essential for healing. Dr. Kristin Neff's research on self-compassion shows that people who practice self-forgiveness are less likely to experience depression and are more resilient to stress.

Conclusion: Forgiveness as a Path to Wholeness

Forgiveness is more than a moral obligation; it is a profound act of healing that restores peace and enables growth. By letting go of resentment, we free ourselves from the mental and emotional burdens that hinder our journey toward wholeness. Whether through prayer, reflection, or therapeutic techniques, the process of forgiveness allows us to step into a life marked by peace, resilience, and spiritual alignment.

Forgiveness, as taught in the Bible, is a gift of divine grace, a powerful act that brings healing to our hearts and souls. As Colossians 3:13 reminds us, "Forgive as the Lord forgave you." Embracing this divine call to forgive allows us to live in freedom and joy, reflecting God's love to others. Through forgiveness, we honor the healing power of grace and set ourselves on a path toward a fuller, more meaningful life.

Faith as a Source of Hope and Resilience

Stories and Teachings on Finding Strength and Solace in a Higher Power During Difficult Times

Introduction: Faith as a Foundation for Resilience and Hope

Life is filled with challenges, and for many, the journey through adversity can be overwhelming. During such times, faith serves as a profound anchor, providing hope, resilience, and a sense of inner peace. The Bible, a rich source of spiritual wisdom, is filled with stories of individuals who found strength through their unwavering trust in God. From the trials of Job to the courage of Esther and Daniel, these narratives remind us that faith can be a source of hope even in the darkest hours.

This chapter explores these stories, drawing lessons and encouragement for facing our own difficulties. By studying these biblical examples, we can find inspiration to persevere, develop resilience, and renew our strength.

1. Job's Resilience Through Faith

The story of Job is perhaps one of the most profound accounts of human suffering and resilience in the Bible. Job was a wealthy and righteous man, known for his deep faith in God. However, in a test of faith and integrity, he lost everything: his wealth, his health, and even his family. In the face of immense loss and suffering, Job's faith was severely tested. Despite his hardships, he refused to curse God, saying, "The Lord gave, and the Lord hath taken away; blessed be the name of the Lord" (Job 1:21, KJV).

Lessons from Job's Perseverance

Job's faith teaches us that resilience is not the absence of suffering but the courage to endure through it. His story reminds us that even when answers are elusive, trust in God can provide comfort and hope. Ultimately, Job's faith was rewarded, as God restored his fortunes and blessed him even more abundantly. His story encourages us to hold onto faith, trusting that even our greatest trials can be a pathway to growth and renewal.

Biblical Support and Concordance Insight

The Hebrew word for "hope" (tikvah) in Job's story represents a cord or anchor, signifying that hope is what holds us steady in turbulent times. Job's example encourages us to cling to hope, trusting that God's plans for us are ultimately for good.

2. The Faith of Daniel: Courage in the Face of Adversity

The story of Daniel is another powerful testament to the resilience of faith. As a young man, Daniel was taken captive to Babylon, where he was forced to live in a foreign land with customs and practices that contradicted his faith.

Despite this, Daniel remained steadfast in his beliefs, refusing to compromise his commitment to God. His unwavering faith even led him to face the lions' den rather than deny his devotion to God.

The Role of Faith in Building Courage

Daniel's story exemplifies how faith can inspire courage and resilience in the face of extreme adversity. Daniel 6:23 (KJV) states, "…no manner of hurt was found upon him, because he believed in his God." His trust in God allowed him to face terrifying circumstances with calm and confidence, knowing that God would deliver him.

Strong Concordance: Faith as a Shield

The Hebrew word for "trust" in Daniel's story, "batach," implies a confident reliance on God's protection. This term emphasizes that faith is like a shield, guarding us from fear and empowering us to confront our challenges with bravery.

3. Esther: A Test of Faith and Sacrifice

The story of Esther, a young Jewish woman who became queen of Persia, illustrates faith as a foundation for bravery and selflessness. When her people were threatened with extermination, Esther courageously approached the king, risking her life to plead for their safety. Her faith and willingness to sacrifice her own safety for others demonstrate the strength and resilience that faith can provide.

Lessons from Esther's Faith

Esther's story reminds us that faith can give us the courage to take bold actions, even when we feel uncertain or fearful. In Esther 4:14 (KJV), her cousin Mordecai tells her, "…who knoweth whether thou art come to the kingdom for such a time as this?" This pivotal moment demonstrates that God places us in specific situations for a purpose, equipping us to face and overcome our challenges.

Theological Insight: Faith as Purpose-Driven Resilience

Esther's story conveys that faith gives us purpose, and with purpose comes resilience. Strong's Concordance highlights the Hebrew word "chayil" (strength or valor) used to describe people who face adversity with inner strength, guided by a divine mission. Her courage provides a timeless reminder of how faith empowers us to face even the most daunting obstacles.

4. Paul's Resilience and Hope Amid Persecution

The Apostle Paul faced significant persecution throughout his ministry. From imprisonment to shipwrecks and even near-death experiences, Paul's journey was one of extreme hardship. Yet, he remained resilient, driven by his unwavering faith in God's purpose for his life. In 2

Corinthians 4:8-9 (KJV), Paul states, "We are troubled on every side, yet not distressed; we are perplexed, but not in despair; persecuted, but not forsaken; cast down, but not destroyed."

Faith as Endurance and Inner Strength

Paul's letters are filled with encouragement and wisdom about enduring hardships through faith. His resilience came from his profound conviction that God was with him, regardless of his circumstances. Paul's example teaches us that faith not only sustains us in adversity but also strengthens our resolve to persevere.

Theological Reflections: Strength Through Christ

Paul's faith-based resilience is encapsulated in Philippians 4:13 (KJV): "I can do all things through Christ which strengtheneth me." Here, Strong's Concordance highlights the Greek word "endunamoó," meaning to empower or give strength, signifying that true resilience comes from divine empowerment rather than mere human will.

5. The Psalmist's Hope in God's Faithfulness

The Book of Psalms is filled with expressions of faith, hope, and resilience in times of distress. The psalmists frequently cried out to God in their suffering, yet they always returned to a message of hope and trust in God's faithfulness.

Psalm 46:1-2 (KJV) declares, "God is our refuge and strength, a very present help in trouble. Therefore will not we fear, though the earth be removed, and though the mountains be carried into the midst of the sea."

Finding Solace in God's Presence

The psalmists' unwavering faith teaches us that resilience can be found in resting in God's presence and trusting in His promises. When life feels overwhelming, faith can offer us a refuge—a place to find peace and hope.

Concordance Insight: The Hebrew Concept of Refuge

The word "refuge" in Hebrew, "machaseh," refers to a shelter or a safe place. The Psalms remind us that faith in God provides not only strength but also a place of spiritual safety, giving us confidence to withstand trials.

6. Practical Steps for Building Faith-Based Resilience

To build resilience through faith, we must actively nurture and cultivate our spiritual life. Here are some practical steps:

a. Regular Prayer and Meditation

Prayer and meditation allow us to connect with God, realign our hearts, and find peace in His presence. These practices strengthen our spiritual foundation, preparing us to face challenges with confidence.

b. Reflect on Biblical Promises

Meditating on verses like Romans 8:28 (KJV) — "And we know that all things work together for good to them that love God" — reminds us of God's unfailing faithfulness, even in difficult times.

c. Surround Yourself with a Faith Community

Being part of a faith community provides a support system and helps build resilience. In fellowship, we can find encouragement, share burdens, and gain strength from others' testimonies of faith.

d. Trust in God's Timing

Resilience often requires patience, trusting that God's timing is perfect. Reflect on Ecclesiastes 3:1 (KJV): "To every thing there is a season, and a time to every purpose under the heaven." Faith can help us remain hopeful, knowing that God's plans for us are good.

Conclusion: Faith as an Anchor in Life's Storms

Faith, when fully embraced, becomes a wellspring of strength, hope, and resilience. The Bible's stories of Job, Daniel, Esther, Paul, and the psalmists offer timeless examples of how faith can empower us to overcome adversity. Through trust in God, we are reminded that no challenge is insurmountable, and no struggle is without purpose. By grounding ourselves in spiritual teachings and cultivating a personal relationship with God, we can draw on a boundless source of resilience that sustains us through all of life's challenges.

CHAPTER 13

BUILDING RESILIENCE AND MOVING FORWARD

Coping Skills for the Long Term

Introduction: The Importance of Building Resilience

Resilience is the ability to bounce back from adversity, adapt to change, and keep moving forward. It is not something we're born with; it is built through practice, experience, and the cultivation of inner strength. By incorporating resilience-building practices into everyday life, we can face life's inevitable challenges with a greater sense of stability and confidence. This chapter explores essential strategies for developing resilience, from nurturing strong relationships and taking care of our physical health to embracing change and building self-confidence.

1. Nurturing Strong Relationships for Support

Relationships are at the core of resilience. Strong, supportive relationships provide us with emotional support, encouragement, and a sense of belonging, especially in times of stress. When we nurture relationships with friends, family, mentors, or support groups, we create a network that we can rely on during difficult times.

Practical Tips

- Seek Open Communication: Being open and honest with others strengthens bonds and promotes trust.

- Cultivate Empathy and Active Listening: Listening actively and empathizing with others improves the quality of relationships.

- Invest in Building Relationships: Spend time with people who uplift and inspire you, and be there for them in return.

2. Taking Care of Your Physical Health

Physical health and mental resilience are closely intertwined. A strong body supports a strong mind, enhancing your ability to cope with stress and recover from challenges. Good nutrition, regular exercise, and adequate sleep are the cornerstones of physical health.

Practical Tips

- Exercise Regularly: Physical activity releases endorphins, the body's natural stress relievers, which improve mood and reduce anxiety.

- Prioritize Sleep: Quality sleep helps regulate mood, increase focus, and enhance mental clarity.

- Eat a Balanced Diet: A nutritious diet fuels both body and mind, giving you the energy to handle life's demands.

3. Finding and Pursuing Your Purpose

Purpose gives life meaning, providing motivation and direction even during difficult times. By finding and focusing on what truly matters to you, you can draw strength from a deeper sense of purpose. This may be found in family, faith, career, creative pursuits, or acts of service.

Practical Tips

- Identify Core Values: Reflect on your personal values, as they often reveal your purpose.

- Set Meaningful Goals: Setting goals aligned with your values helps you stay focused and resilient.

- Volunteer or Help Others: Serving others can help give perspective, purpose, and fulfillment, reinforcing your resilience.

4. Embracing Change

Change is a constant in life, and learning to accept it is key to resilience. Resilient individuals view change not as a threat but as an opportunity for growth and learning. Embracing change helps you adapt more easily and bounce back from setbacks.

Practical Tips

- Practice Flexibility: Be open to new ideas, experiences, and viewpoints.

- Shift from a Fixed to a Growth Mindset: View challenges as opportunities to learn rather than as obstacles.

- Break Down Change into Steps: Approach change gradually by breaking it into manageable parts, reducing feelings of overwhelm.

5. Building Self-Confidence

Confidence in your own abilities allows you to approach problems with a proactive mindset. Building self-confidence means recognizing your strengths, acknowledging past successes, and believing in your capacity to overcome future challenges.

Practical Tips

- Celebrate Small Wins: Acknowledge your achievements, no matter how small. This builds a sense of accomplishment.

- Challenge Negative Self-Talk: Replace self-doubt with affirmations and positive thoughts.

- Set and Achieve Small Goals: Start with small goals and work your way up to bigger challenges. Success breeds confidence.

6. Maintaining Perspective in Difficult Situations

Resilient individuals maintain perspective by keeping the bigger picture in mind. They remind themselves that challenges are temporary and that they have the power to overcome them. Maintaining perspective helps reduce stress and prevent the feeling of being overwhelmed.

Practical Tips

- Practice Gratitude: Regularly listing things you are grateful for shifts focus from problems to positive aspects of life.

- Avoid Catastrophic Thinking: When facing challenges, avoid imagining the worst-case scenario. Try to look at situations objectively.

- Take Breaks: Giving yourself time to step back from a problem allows you to return with a fresh perspective.

7. Developing Problem-Solving Skills

Problem-solving is an essential part of resilience. By learning to assess and solve problems effectively, you develop a sense of agency, which reinforces resilience and helps you feel more in control.

Practical Tips

- Break Down Problems: Divide larger problems into smaller, more manageable parts.

- Brainstorm Solutions: Generate multiple solutions and evaluate the pros and cons of each.

- Take Decisive Action: Commit to a solution and take action, even if it's just a small step. This keeps you moving forward.

8. Learning Effective Stress Management Techniques

Effective stress management reduces the impact of difficult situations on your mental and physical well-being. Building resilience means equipping yourself with tools to cope with stress healthily and productively.

Practical Tips

- Practice Mindfulness and Meditation: These practices help reduce stress and enhance focus, grounding you in the present.

- Engage in Relaxing Activities: Find activities that relax you, whether reading, listening to music, gardening, or spending time in nature.

- Use Deep Breathing Exercises: Deep breathing activates the body's relaxation response, helping to reduce anxiety and calm the mind.

Integrating Resilience-Building Practices into Daily Life

Building resilience isn't about applying these techniques sporadically; it's about making them part of your daily routine. Incorporate small habits gradually, focusing on one or two practices at a time. Over time, these practices will become second nature, allowing you to cultivate resilience in a sustainable way.

Sample Daily Routine

- Morning: Begin with a few minutes of mindfulness or meditation, setting an intention for the day.

- Throughout the Day: Practice gratitude and maintain perspective by focusing on what you can control.

- Evening: Reflect on your day, celebrate small wins, and acknowledge any challenges you faced positively.

Conclusion: Moving Forward with Resilience

Resilience is built through intentional action and the consistent application of strategies that nurture both body and mind. By focusing on supportive relationships, caring for physical health, finding purpose, embracing change, and building confidence, you can enhance your resilience and face life's challenges with a renewed sense of strength. Remember, resilience is not about eliminating difficulty from life but about developing the capacity to navigate challenges with grace and perseverance. With a strong foundation, you can move forward, overcoming adversity and finding fulfillment even in the face of life's most difficult circumstances.

Setting Goals and Finding Purpose

Creating a Life of Meaning, Hope, and Self-Compassion

Introduction: The Power of Purpose

Purpose is the driving force that gives life meaning. It's what makes us feel fulfilled, and it motivates us to get out of bed every morning. As the Cambridge Dictionary defines it, purpose is "why you do something or why something exists." In the context of our lives, purpose is what gives us a sense of direction. It's that sense of meaning, whether large or small, that guides us and helps us make choices that align with our true selves.

Purpose can take many forms. For some, it's found in their families, their work, or their creative pursuits. For others, it's about helping others, contributing to the world, or growing spiritually. Finding purpose is deeply personal, yet essential for everyone. It gives us resilience, hope, and self-compassion, providing a foundation for setting meaningful goals and building a fulfilling life.

1. Understanding the Concept of Purpose

For many, "finding purpose" can feel like an overwhelming or even abstract idea. Yet, purpose is often closer than we think. It's in the small, everyday things that make us feel connected, motivated, and alive. Purpose isn't always about grand gestures or large-scale impact; rather, it's about finding something that resonates deeply within us.

Purpose answers two questions:

1. Who am I?

2. What am I here to contribute?

These questions are at the heart of discovering what matters most to us. While these questions might seem daunting, discovering purpose doesn't necessarily involve one defining moment or big decision. It's an ongoing process that involves reflection, exploration, and growth.

2. Why Finding Purpose is Essential for Mental Well-Being

Having a purpose is like having an internal compass that helps us navigate through life's storms. Research shows that people who have a sense of purpose are more resilient, less likely to experience depression, and more satisfied with life. Purpose provides hope, direction, and a reason to keep going when things get tough.

The Role of Purpose in Coping with Adversity

Purpose serves as an anchor during challenging times. When life becomes difficult, having something to focus on and work toward can provide comfort and motivation. For example, someone facing a personal loss may find purpose in supporting others going through similar experiences. By helping others, they channel their own pain into something constructive and meaningful.

The Link Between Purpose and Self-Compassion

Purpose also fosters self-compassion. When we have a purpose, we can see ourselves as individuals with value, contributing something meaningful to the world. This helps us extend kindness to ourselves, particularly when we face setbacks or failures, recognizing that our journey is part of something bigger.

3. Finding Purpose: A Journey, Not a Destination

Purpose is often something we discover gradually, through experiences and reflections rather than all at once. It involves exploring our interests, understanding our values, and considering what brings us joy and fulfillment. Some of the most effective ways to find purpose include self-reflection, exploring different activities, and staying open to new experiences.

Practical Steps to Discover Your Purpose

1. Reflect on Your Values: What do you care about most deeply? These values can be a powerful clue to your purpose.

2. Think About What Energizes You: Pay attention to activities or topics that make you feel alive or passionate.

3. Explore Areas Where You Can Make a Difference: Purpose often involves contributing to something greater than ourselves, even if it's on a small scale.

4. Ask Yourself What You Want to Be Remembered For: Imagine how you'd like to be remembered. What qualities or actions would you like people to associate with you?

Example

Consider someone who has always enjoyed teaching and sharing knowledge. This enjoyment might hint at a purpose rooted in educating others, whether as a teacher, a mentor, or simply a supportive friend.

4. Setting Goals Aligned with Your Purpose

Once you have a sense of your purpose, setting goals can help you bring it to life in practical ways. Goals transform purpose into achievable, actionable steps, giving us a roadmap for making our purpose a reality.

How to Set Purpose-Driven Goals

1. Identify Long-Term Goals: Consider what you hope to achieve over the next several years that aligns with your purpose.

2. Break Down Goals into Short-Term Milestones: Large goals can be overwhelming; breaking them into smaller, achievable steps makes them more manageable.

3. Stay Flexible: Purpose-driven goals should be adaptable. If your circumstances or priorities change, don't be afraid to adjust your goals accordingly.

Example of Purpose-Driven Goals

If your purpose is to help others, you might set goals like volunteering regularly, pursuing a career in a helping profession, or even mentoring someone.

5. Practical Techniques for Living a Purposeful Life

Purpose is not only something to be discovered but also nurtured. Here are some techniques to help you live with purpose every day:

1. Mindful Reflection: Spend time each day reflecting on your actions and thoughts. Ask yourself if they align with your purpose.

2. Practice Gratitude: Gratitude helps reinforce the positive aspects of your purpose, reminding you of the reasons you feel motivated.

3. Engage in Activities Aligned with Your Values: Fill your time with activities that support your purpose and bring you joy.

4. Surround Yourself with Supportive People: Relationships with those who support and encourage your purpose can keep you focused and motivated.

6. The Importance of Self-Compassion on the Journey to Purpose

Pursuing a purpose can sometimes be challenging, and there will likely be setbacks along the way. Cultivating self-compassion is essential for maintaining your purpose. When things don't go as planned, self-compassion allows you to treat yourself with kindness and understanding, rather than self-criticism.

How to Practice Self-Compassion

- Forgive Yourself for Mistakes: Remind yourself that mistakes are part of the journey and opportunities for growth.

- Take Care of Your Emotional Needs: Prioritize self-care practices that recharge you emotionally.

- Encourage Yourself with Positive Self-Talk: Use affirmations to build self-esteem and remind yourself of your value.

7. Overcoming Obstacles to Purpose

Finding and following your purpose isn't always easy. Obstacles may include self-doubt, fear of failure, or feeling that others might not support your journey. Overcoming these challenges often requires resilience, self-belief, and the willingness to take risks.

Strategies for Overcoming Obstacles

1. Identify Limiting Beliefs: Recognize beliefs that hold you back, such as "I'm not good enough" or "It's too late to change."

2. Build Resilience: Approach challenges as opportunities to grow and learn rather than as setbacks.

3. Seek Support: Finding people who believe in your purpose can provide the encouragement and motivation needed to keep going.

8. Purpose and Meaning in Daily Life: Small Steps with Big Impact

Purpose doesn't always involve big decisions or life-altering changes. Often, purpose is found in small, everyday actions that reflect our values and intentions. Small moments of kindness, small contributions, and small steps toward our goals can create a fulfilling sense of purpose.

Examples of Purposeful Daily Practices

- Helping a Colleague: Assisting a coworker or offering encouragement reflects purpose and meaning in your daily work.

- Practicing Mindfulness: Living in the present moment enhances your ability to appreciate small, purposeful actions.

- Expressing Gratitude: Showing appreciation to people around you strengthens relationships and builds a supportive environment.

9. Conclusion: Moving Forward with a Sense of Purpose

Setting goals and finding purpose is a journey that requires self-reflection, commitment, and compassion. With a clear sense of purpose, we can face life's challenges with resilience, find joy in our accomplishments, and create a meaningful life. Each step forward brings us closer to a life of meaning, hope, and self-compassion. As you continue to explore your purpose and set meaningful goals, remember that the journey itself is just as valuable as the destination. With purpose as your guide, you have the power to transform your life, enriching both your experience and the lives of those around you.

Renewed Faith and a Hopeful Outlook

Reflections on Spiritual Growth, Finding Peace, and Believing in the Possibility of a Fulfilling Future

Introduction: Embracing a Journey of Spiritual Renewal

Faith, hope, and peace are foundational to a fulfilling life, especially when we face challenges and uncertainties. Spiritual renewal isn't a one-time event but a continuous journey that draws us closer to God, transforming our hearts and minds. The Bible offers numerous practices to help Christians pursue spiritual renewal and develop a hopeful outlook: prayer, repentance, Scripture study, worship, fasting, accountability, service, forgiveness, thankfulness, resting in God, seeking the Holy Spirit, and self-reflection. By integrating these disciplines, believers can nurture a resilient faith, cultivate inner peace, and trust in God's promises for a fulfilling future.

1. The Role of Prayer in Spiritual Renewal

Prayer is the foundation of a renewed faith, as it establishes an intimate connection with God. Through prayer, we express gratitude, seek guidance, and find solace, bringing our struggles and joys before Him. The Bible encourages believers to "pray without ceasing" (1 Thessalonians 5:17) as a way to maintain a constant awareness of God's presence.

Key Aspects of Prayer

- Thanksgiving: Offering gratitude for God's blessings strengthens faith and shifts focus from challenges to God's goodness (Philippians 4:6-7).

- Petition: Asking for God's help acknowledges our dependence on Him and opens our hearts to receive His guidance.

- Intercession: Praying for others fosters compassion and reminds us that we're part of a larger community of faith.

Reflective Practice: Set aside dedicated time daily for prayer, cultivating a habit of communion with God. Write down specific prayers and reflect on how God answers them over time, building a record of His faithfulness.

2. The Power of Repentance and Forgiveness

Repentance involves recognizing and turning away from sin, seeking God's forgiveness and grace. The act of repentance renews our spirits by freeing us from guilt and strengthening our relationship with God. As 1 John 1:9 reminds us, "If we confess our sins, He is faithful and just to forgive us our sins and to cleanse us from all unrighteousness."

Forgiveness is equally transformative. Jesus taught that forgiving others is essential to receiving God's forgiveness (Matthew 6:14-15). By releasing resentment and choosing forgiveness, we let go of burdens that can otherwise hinder our spiritual growth and peace.

Reflective Practice: Regularly examine your heart, confessing any sins and asking God to help you forgive others. Keep a journal of any experiences or changes in perspective that occur as you practice repentance and forgiveness.

3. Engaging with Scripture for Deeper Understanding

Studying the Bible is central to spiritual renewal, as it reveals God's character, promises, and guidance for living a life of faith. Hebrews 4:12 describes Scripture as "alive and active," able to reach the depths of our souls and transform us. By meditating on God's Word, believers find wisdom, encouragement, and strength to navigate life's challenges.

Practical Approaches to Scripture Study

- Daily Reading: Read a passage daily and ask God to reveal insights or lessons.

- Meditation: Reflect deeply on specific verses or themes, allowing them to resonate in your heart.

- Application: Consider how each Scripture can be applied practically in your life.

Reflective Practice: Select a verse each week to meditate on and memorize, and allow it to shape your actions and thoughts.

4. Worship as an Expression of Faith and Gratitude

Worship is a powerful way to draw near to God, offering Him praise and acknowledging His sovereignty. Worship not only brings us closer to God but also reminds us of His greatness, filling us with awe and gratitude. The psalmist writes, "Come, let us bow down in worship, let us kneel before the Lord our Maker" (Psalm 95:6). In worship, we express our deepest reverence and love for God, strengthening our spiritual foundation.

Reflective Practice: Incorporate worship into your daily routine, whether through music, singing, or silent praise. Let worship be an intentional time to focus solely on God's glory and goodness.

5. Fasting for Clarity and Spiritual Discipline

Fasting is a spiritual practice that fosters humility, discipline, and reliance on God. By voluntarily giving up certain comforts, we open space to focus on God's presence and purpose. In Matthew 6:16-18, Jesus speaks about fasting with sincerity, not for public recognition but as an offering to God. Fasting renews our spirit by drawing us closer to God and helping us prioritize Him above all else.

Reflective Practice: Consider a regular fast, whether from food, technology, or other distractions, using the time to pray and reflect on God's purpose for your life.

6. Accountability and Fellowship in the Faith Community

Accountability in fellowship is vital for spiritual growth. Ecclesiastes 4:9-10 teaches that "two are better than one" because they can support and encourage each other.

Being part of a faith community provides a network of support, encouragement, and guidance. Through fellowship, we gain strength and motivation to remain steadfast in our spiritual walk.

Reflective Practice: Find a trusted friend or group in your community to share your spiritual journey, challenges, and victories. Allow others to encourage you and offer guidance as you pursue spiritual renewal.

7. The Power of Service: Finding Purpose through Helping Others

Service to others is both a commandment and a means to experience spiritual renewal. Jesus modeled this in His life, teaching, "Just as the Son of Man did not come to be served, but to serve" (Matthew 20:28). Serving others shifts our focus from our own challenges to the needs around us, allowing us to live out our faith in tangible ways. Through service, we align ourselves with God's love and compassion, finding renewed purpose.

Reflective Practice: Identify ways to serve in your community, such as volunteering or offering support to those in need. Reflect on how each act of service brings you closer to God's heart.

8. Practicing Thankfulness as a Path to Peace

Gratitude is a powerful practice that fosters contentment and shifts our focus from lack to abundance. By cultivating thankfulness, we remind ourselves of God's faithfulness and provision. The Apostle Paul encourages us in 1 Thessalonians 5:18 to "give thanks in all circumstances," trusting that God is present in every season of life.

Reflective Practice: Each day, write down three things you're grateful for, focusing on God's blessings, both large and small. Over time, this practice builds a mindset of peace and contentment.

9. Resting in God's Presence for Renewal

Rest is essential for both physical and spiritual renewal. In Matthew 11:28, Jesus invites us to come to Him for rest, saying, "Come to me, all you who are weary and burdened, and I will give you rest." Resting in God's presence allows us to let go of our worries, trusting in His care. This practice renews our spirit, giving us the strength to face each day with peace and hope.

Reflective Practice: Dedicate time each week for quiet reflection, turning off distractions and resting in God's presence through prayer or silent meditation.

10. Seeking the Guidance of the Holy Spirit

The Holy Spirit is our divine Helper, leading us in truth and empowering us to live out our faith. Jesus promised the Holy Spirit to His followers, saying, "But the Advocate, the Holy Spirit, whom the Father will send in my name, will teach you all things" (John 14:26). Relying on the Holy Spirit provides wisdom, comfort, and insight as we navigate life's challenges.

Reflective Practice: Start each day by asking the Holy Spirit to guide your actions and decisions. Listen for His promptings and trust in His presence as you go about your day.

11. Self-Reflection: Examining Your Heart and Mind

Self-reflection is crucial for spiritual growth. By regularly examining our thoughts, attitudes, and actions, we can align ourselves more closely with God's will. Lamentations 3:40 says, "Let us examine our ways and test them, and let us return to the Lord." This practice helps us identify areas where we need growth, fostering spiritual maturity.

Reflective Practice: At the end of each day, spend time reflecting on your actions and thoughts. Consider if they align with God's teachings, and ask for His guidance in areas of improvement.

Conclusion: Building a Hopeful Outlook through Spiritual Growth

Spiritual renewal is an ongoing journey that strengthens faith, deepens peace, and builds resilience. By embracing practices such as prayer, repentance, Scripture study, and worship, we open our hearts to God's transformative power. This renewal fosters a hopeful outlook, allowing us to face life's challenges with trust and joy. In God's presence, we find purpose, strength, and the assurance of a fulfilling future, grounded in His unwavering love and faithfulness.

CONCLUSION

EMBRACING A JOURNEY OF HEALING

Healing from depression is a journey, one that requires patience, compassion, and commitment. Throughout this book, we have explored various paths to understanding and overcoming depression, from scientific approaches to spiritual practices. Healing doesn't happen overnight; it unfolds gradually as we incorporate each aspect of care—physical, mental, emotional, and spiritual—into our lives.

Depression is complex, affecting not just the mind but the entire person, and so it calls for a holistic approach. We've looked at practical ways to care for mental health, such as through cognitive-behavioral therapy, goal-setting, and resilience-building techniques. Each strategy plays a role in challenging negative thoughts, building positive habits, and finding meaning and purpose in life. We've also explored the deep connection between body and mind, examining the importance of nutrition, physical health, and even sunlight in lifting our mood and improving overall well-being.

Yet, healing is not only about taking action but also about being gentle with ourselves. Cultivating a hopeful mindset and practicing self-compassion can transform how we experience struggles. Embracing faith and spirituality, as we've discussed, brings an inner peace that science alone may not provide. Turning to prayer, forgiveness, worship, and other spiritual practices helps us connect with a higher power, offering comfort, strength, and renewed purpose. Biblical teachings remind us that even in the darkest valleys, we are not alone, and that faith can serve as an anchor, grounding us through life's storms.

Reaching out for support—whether through friends, family, or a professional counselor—is an essential step. Healing is seldom a solo journey; it is enriched by the connections we have with others. Surrounding ourselves with people who encourage and uplift us, and building supportive relationships, can be one of the most powerful sources of hope and resilience.

As you continue on this journey of healing, may you find comfort in knowing that each step forward, however small, brings you closer to a fulfilling life. Remember that setbacks are natural and do not negate progress. Embrace each day as an opportunity for growth, and trust that healing is possible. With patience, openness, and faith, you can build a future filled with peace, joy, and renewed strength in both mind and spirit.